Tunisian Cookbook
Authentic Recipes

UNCOVER THE RICH AND DIVERSE FLAVORS OF TUNISIA

FATIMA M. SALAH

TUNISIAN COOKBOOK
Uncover the Rich and Diverse Flavors of Tunisia.

© Fatima M. Salah
© E.G.P. Editorial
   ISBN-13: 9798882695117

Copyright © 2024
All rights reserved.

FLAVOURS THAT CROSS BORDERS

From my earliest memories, the tales of Tunisia and the resonant sounds of traditional music filled the air, forging a profound bond with my heritage, even as we were miles away from my grandmother's native land. My grandmother, a symbol of resilience and optimism, together with my grandfather, decided in the 1950s that New York would become their new abode, a place to chase better opportunities for their descendants, melding into the vibrant and diverse Tunisian community in Brooklyn.

The decision to traverse seas and establish roots in a foreign territory was formidable; yet, my grandmother's steadfast courage and hopeful perspective never wavered. Her stories infused me with the importance of maintaining our cultural and traditional ties alive, particularly through culinary arts. My grandmother's kitchen was transformed into a sanctuary of scents and tastes, not just preparing meals for nourishment but as a means of soulful connection, bridging us with our Tunisian heritage.

My grandmother impressed upon me that cooking is more than the simple act of food preparation; it is an act of love, a way to conserve our heritage and share our narratives with the coming generations. Each recipe she handed down was steeped in a tale, a teaching, or a reminiscence of Tunisia, turning every meal into a festivity of our identity.

The role of Tunisian cuisine in my life was profoundly influenced by my grandmother's teachings and further enriched by literature of the era that celebrated the richness and diversity of our culinary legacy. These works were crucial for my grandmother to perfect and hone her recipes, which became the centerpiece of our family gatherings in New York.

Now, as an adult and the author of this book, my goal is to safeguard and propagate my grandmother's culinary legacy. Though she has passed, her spirit and wisdom continue to guide me each time I prepare one of her dishes. This book is a homage to her, to her life filled with strength, love, and a passion for cooking, aiming to inspire others to discover the joy and unity found in the culinary arts.

Through this book, I wish for readers to not only learn to create authentic Tunisian dishes but also to immerse themselves in the love and dedication my grandmother put into each recipe. Let this book serve as a bridge between generations and cultures, illustrating that, no matter where we are, cooking can offer a haven for both heart and soul.

TABLE OF CONTENTS

SPICES AND PANTRY 9
APPETIZERS 16
SALADS 29
SOUPS 41
STEWS 55
SEAFOOD 70
POULTRY 84
LAMB DISHES 104
BEEF DISHES 123
GRAIN DISHES 141
DESSERTS 159
RECIPE LIST 179

SPICES & PANTRY

The spices and pantry staples of Tunisian cuisine offer a rich tapestry of flavors that are both distinctive and essential to its dishes. These elements, from the fiery heat of harissa to the aromatic blend of ras el hanout, provide depth and complexity to each meal, setting Tunisian culinary traditions apart from others. Their use not only enhances the sensory experience of dining but also brings numerous health benefits, including anti-inflammatory and antioxidant properties that are pivotal for a nutritious diet.

Tunisian cuisine's pantry is a testament to its versatility and adaptability, incorporating a variety of grains, legumes, and preserved foods that are fundamental to its dishes. This diversity allows for a wide range of culinary creations, from simple, everyday meals to elaborate, festive dishes, all while adhering to principles of healthy eating. The strategic use of these spices and staples underscores the cuisine's ability to merge traditional flavors with nutritional needs, offering dishes that are both wholesome and satisfying.

Moreover, the emphasis on spices and pantry essentials in Tunisian cooking highlights the cuisine's commitment to flavor-rich and health-conscious food preparation. Through the careful selection and combination of these ingredients, Tunisian cuisine showcases its dedication to fostering a dining experience that nourishes the body and delights the palate.

HARISSA

Ingredients

- Chili peppers - 10, dried and deseeded.
- Garlic cloves - 3, peeled.
- Coriander seeds - 1 tsp.
- Caraway seeds - 1/2 tsp.
- Salt - 1 tsp.
- Olive oil - 3 tbsp.

Instructions

1. Soak the dried chili peppers in hot water for 30 minutes to soften.

2. Drain the peppers and blend with garlic, coriander seeds, caraway seeds, and salt until smooth.

3. Gradually blend in olive oil until a paste forms.

4. Store in an airtight container in the refrigerator.

RAS EL HANOUT

Ingredients

- Coriander seeds - 1 tbsp.
- Cumin seeds - 1 tbsp.
- Cinnamon stick - 1, broken into pieces.
- Cardamom pods - 6.
- Cloves - 6.
- Nutmeg - 1/4 tsp, grated.
- Turmeric powder - 1 tsp.

Instructions

1. Toast the coriander seeds, cumin seeds, cinnamon stick, cardamom pods, and cloves in a dry pan until fragrant.

2. Cool and grind the toasted spices with nutmeg and turmeric to a fine powder.

3. Store in an airtight container away from direct sunlight.

TABIL

Ingredients

- Coriander seeds - 2 tbsp.
- Caraway seeds - 1 tbsp.
- Garlic powder - 1 tsp.
- Dried chili flakes - 1 tsp.

Instructions

1. Toast the coriander and caraway seeds in a dry pan until fragrant.

2. Grind the toasted seeds with garlic powder and chili flakes to a fine powder.

3. Store in an airtight container away from direct sunlight.

CHERMOULA

Ingredients

- Fresh cilantro - 1 cup, chopped.

- Fresh parsley - 1 cup, chopped.
- Garlic cloves - 3, minced.
- Cumin - 1 tsp.
- Paprika - 1 tsp.
- Lemon juice - 2 tbsp.
- Olive oil - 1/4 cup.
- Salt - to taste.

Instructions

1. Combine cilantro, parsley, garlic, cumin, paprika, lemon juice, and salt in a blender.

2. Blend while gradually adding olive oil until a smooth paste forms.

3. Adjust salt to taste and store in an airtight container in the refrigerator.

BZAR (TUNISIAN SPICE MIX)

Ingredients

- Coriander seeds - 2 tbsp.
- Caraway seeds - 1 tbsp.
- Dried chili flakes - 1 tbsp.
- Garlic powder - 1 tsp.
- Salt - 1/2 tsp.

Instructions

1. Toast coriander seeds, caraway seeds, and dried chili flakes in a dry pan until fragrant.

2. Grind the toasted spices with garlic powder and salt to a fine powder.

3. Store in an airtight container away from direct sunlight.

DRIED MINT

Ingredients

- Fresh mint leaves - 1 bunch.

Instructions

1. Rinse the mint leaves and pat dry with a towel.

2. Arrange the leaves on a baking sheet in a single layer.

3. Place the baking sheet in a warm, dry area away from direct sunlight and allow the leaves to air dry for 1-2 weeks, or until completely dry and brittle.

4. Crumble the dried leaves and store in an airtight container away from light.

CARAWAY POWDER

Ingredients

- Caraway seeds - 1 cup.

Instructions

1. Toast the caraway seeds in a dry skillet over medium heat until fragrant, about 2-3 minutes, stirring constantly.

2. Allow the seeds to cool completely.

3. Grind the toasted seeds to a fine powder using a spice grinder or mortar and pestle.

4. Store the caraway powder in an airtight container away from light and heat.

CORIANDER SEEDS

Ingredients

- Coriander seeds - 1 cup.

Instructions

1. Toast the coriander seeds in a dry skillet over medium heat until fragrant, about 2-3 minutes, stirring constantly.

2. Allow the seeds to cool completely.

3. Store the toasted coriander seeds in an airtight container away from light and heat, or grind to a powder if desired.

SMEN (CLARIFIED BUTTER)

Ingredients

- Unsalted butter - 1 kg.

Instructions

1. Melt the unsalted butter in a saucepan over low heat, allowing it to simmer gently until the milk solids separate and settle at the bottom.

2. Skim off the foam that rises to the top.

3. Carefully pour the clear butterfat into a clean container, leaving the milk solids behind.

4. Allow the smen to cool and solidify. Store in an airtight container in a cool, dark place.

PRESERVED LEMONS

Ingredients

- Lemons - 10, preferably organic.
- Sea salt - 1/2 cup.

Instructions

1. Scrub the lemons clean and cut them into quarters, leaving the base intact so the lemons are still connected at the bottom.

2. Open up the lemons and generously sprinkle salt inside.

3. Pack the lemons tightly in a sterilized jar, pressing them down to release their juices and cover them with lemon juice if necessary. Top with an additional layer of salt.

4. Seal the jar and leave in a cool, dark place for at least 3 weeks, turning the jar upside down occasionally to distribute the salt and juices.

5. Once preserved, the lemons can be refrigerated and used for up to a year.

APPETIZERS

Tunisian appetizers stand out in the culinary world for their rich blend of flavors and healthful ingredients. These starters, often vibrant with spices and fresh produce, set the stage for a dining experience that is both nutritious and tantalizing to the palate. They embody the essence of Tunisian cuisine, which masterfully balances taste and health benefits, showcasing the country's abundant Mediterranean harvest.

The versatility of Tunisian appetizers is unmatched, serving not just as mere precursors to the main course but as a showcase of the culinary diversity that Tunisia offers. From light and refreshing salads to hearty, spice-infused small plates, these dishes are designed to cater to a wide array of dietary preferences and eating habits. They are a testament to the adaptability of Tunisian cuisine, easily integrating into a healthy eating regimen without sacrificing flavor.

Furthermore, Tunisian appetizers contribute significantly to a balanced diet. Rich in vegetables, legumes, and grains, they are a source of essential nutrients and fiber, supporting overall health and well-being. Through these carefully crafted dishes, Tunisian cuisine invites diners to explore a world where gastronomy and nutrition harmoniously intersect.

BRIK À L'ŒUF

Ingredients

- Warka pastry sheets - 4.
- Eggs - 4.
- Tuna - 1 can, drained.

- Capres - 1 tablespoon.
- Parsley - 1 tablespoon, chopped.
- Harissa - 1 teaspoon.
- Salt - to taste.
- Vegetable oil - for frying.

Instructions

1. Place a warka pastry sheet on a flat surface and add a portion of the tuna, capers, parsley, and a small amount of harissa in the center.

2. Make a well in the center of the filling and carefully crack an egg into it. Season with salt.

3. Fold the pastry over the filling to create a half-moon shape, sealing the edges by pressing them together.

4. Heat oil in a frying pan over medium heat and fry the brik on both sides until golden brown.

5. Serve immediately.

MECHOUIA SALAD

Ingredients

- Bell peppers - 3, mixed colors.
- Tomatoes - 2.
- Garlic cloves - 2.
- Onion - 1, small.
- Olive oil - 2 tablespoons.
- Lemon juice - 1 tablespoon.
- Salt and black pepper - to taste.
- Olives and capers - for garnish.

Instructions

1. Roast the bell peppers, tomatoes, garlic, and onion in the oven or over an open flame until charred.

2. Peel the charred skin off the vegetables and chop them finely.

3. Mix the chopped vegetables in a bowl with olive oil and lemon juice. Season with salt and pepper.

4. Garnish with olives and capers before serving.

TUNISIAN FELFEL (ROASTED PEPPERS)

Ingredients

- Bell peppers - 4, various colors.
- Garlic cloves - 2, minced.
- Olive oil - 2 tablespoons.
- Caraway seeds - 1 teaspoon, ground.
- Coriander seeds - 1 teaspoon, ground.
- Salt and pepper - to taste.
- Lemon juice - 1 tablespoon.

Instructions

1. Roast the bell peppers until their skin blisters and blackens.

2. Place the roasted peppers in a bowl and cover with plastic wrap to steam for 10 minutes, then peel off the skin.

3. Chop the peppers and mix with the garlic, olive oil, ground caraway, ground coriander, salt, pepper, and lemon juice.

4. Serve chilled or at room temperature.

ZAALOUK

Ingredients

- Eggplants - 2, medium.
- Tomatoes - 3, peeled and chopped.
- Garlic cloves - 2, minced.
- Paprika - 1 teaspoon.
- Cumin - 1 teaspoon.
- Olive oil - 3 tablespoons.
- Cilantro - 1/4 cup, chopped.
- Lemon juice - 1 tablespoon.
- Salt and pepper - to taste.

Instructions

1. Roast the eggplants until tender, then peel and mash the flesh.

2. In a pan, heat the olive oil and sauté the garlic, paprika, and cumin for a minute.

3. Add the tomatoes and cook until soft.

4. Mix in the mashed eggplant, cilantro, lemon juice, salt, and pepper. Cook for 10 minutes, stirring occasionally.

5. Serve warm or cold, garnished with extra cilantro.

LABLABI

Ingredients

- Chickpeas - 2 cups, soaked overnight and drained.
- Garlic cloves - 3, minced.
- Ground cumin - 1 teaspoon.
- Olive oil - 2 tablespoons.
- Harissa paste - 1 tablespoon.
- Lemon juice - from 1 lemon.
- Salt and pepper - to taste.
- Crusty bread - for serving.

Instructions

1. In a large pot, cover the chickpeas with water and bring to a boil. Reduce heat and simmer until tender, about 1 hour.

2. In a skillet, heat the olive oil over medium heat. Add the garlic and cumin, and cook until fragrant.

3. Add the garlic and cumin mixture to the chickpeas, along with the harissa, lemon juice, salt, and pepper.

4. Serve the lablabi hot over torn pieces of crusty bread.

TUNISIAN SAMSA

Ingredients

- Almonds - 300 grams, finely ground.
- Phyllo pastry - 10 sheets.
- Butter - 100 grams, melted.
- Powdered sugar - 150 grams.
- Cinnamon powder - 1 teaspoon.
- Orange flower water - 2 tablespoons.

- Honey - 200 grams, for syrup.

Instructions

1. Combine ground almonds, powdered sugar, cinnamon, and orange flower water in a bowl to make the filling.

2. Cut phyllo sheets into strips, place a small amount of filling at one end, and fold into triangles, brushing with melted butter.

3. Bake in a preheated oven at 180°C (356°F) until golden, about 15-20 minutes.

4. Warm honey in a saucepan and dip the baked samsa into it. Let them soak for a few minutes before removing.

KAFTEJI

Ingredients

- Potatoes - 2, diced.
- Carrots - 2, diced.
- Zucchini - 1, diced.
- Pumpkin - 200 grams, diced.
- Eggs - 4.
- Vegetable oil - for frying.
- Harissa - 1 tablespoon.
- Garlic - 2 cloves, minced.
- Lemon juice - 2 tablespoons.

Instructions

1. Fry diced potatoes, carrots, zucchini, and pumpkin in vegetable oil until golden and crispy.

2. Drain the vegetables on paper towels to remove excess oil.

3. In a large bowl, mix the fried vegetables with harissa, minced garlic, and lemon juice.

4. In a frying pan, fry the eggs to your preference and place them on top of the vegetable mix.

MERGUEZ SAUSAGE

Ingredients

- Merguez sausages - 500 grams.
- Vegetable oil - 1 tablespoon.

Instructions

1. Heat vegetable oil in a frying pan over medium heat.

2. Add merguez sausages and cook for about 10 minutes, turning occasionally until evenly browned and cooked through. Serve hot with bread and a side of salad.

TUNISIAN BOUREK

Ingredients

- Thin pastry sheets - 10.
- Minced meat - 500 grams (beef or lamb).
- Onion - 1, finely chopped.
- Parsley - ½ cup, chopped.
- Cheddar cheese - 100 grams, grated.
- Eggs - 3.
- Salt and pepper - to taste.
- Oil - for frying.

Instructions

1. Cook the minced meat with chopped onion, salt, and pepper until fully cooked. Let it cool.

2. Add chopped parsley, grated cheese, and eggs to the meat mixture and combine well.

3. Place a tablespoon of the filling on each pastry sheet, fold the edges, and roll tightly.

4. Fry in hot oil until golden brown on all sides.

5. Drain on paper towels before serving.

HMISS

Ingredients

- Red peppers - 4, roasted and peeled.
- Tomatoes - 2, roasted, peeled, and chopped.
- Garlic cloves - 2, minced.
- Caraway seeds - ½ teaspoon, crushed.
- Coriander seeds - ½ teaspoon, crushed.
- Olives - ¼ cup, sliced.
- Olive oil - 2 tablespoons.
- Lemon juice - 1 tablespoon.
- Salt and pepper - to taste.

Instructions

1. Chop the roasted red peppers into small pieces.

2. In a bowl, combine the roasted red peppers, chopped tomatoes, minced garlic, crushed caraway and coriander seeds, sliced olives, olive oil, lemon juice, salt, and pepper.

3. Mix well and adjust seasoning to taste.

4. Serve chilled or at room temperature as an appetizer or side dish.

MAKROUD EL LOUSE

Ingredients

- Almond flour - 500 grams.
- Powdered sugar - 300 grams.
- Butter - 100 grams, melted.
- Orange blossom water - 3 tablespoons.
- Whole almonds - for decoration.

Instructions

1. Mix almond flour and powdered sugar in a bowl.

2. Gradually add melted butter and orange blossom water, kneading until the mixture becomes a smooth dough.

3. Shape the dough into small balls, pressing an almond into the top of each one.

4. Arrange on a baking sheet and bake at 160°C (320°F) for 10-15 minutes or until set but not browned.

5. Let cool before serving.

TAKTOUKA

Ingredients

- Bell peppers - 2, roasted and peeled.
- Tomatoes - 3, peeled and finely chopped.

- Garlic cloves - 2, minced.
- Olive oil - 2 tablespoons.
- Ground cumin - 1 teaspoon.
- Paprika - 1 teaspoon.
- Salt and pepper - to taste.
- Fresh cilantro - 2 tablespoons, chopped.

Instructions

1. Chop the roasted bell peppers finely.

2. Heat olive oil in a pan and sauté garlic until fragrant.

3. Add tomatoes, bell peppers, cumin, paprika, salt, and pepper to the pan. Cook until the mixture thickens.

4. Stir in chopped cilantro just before removing from heat.

5. Serve warm or cold as a side dish or appetizer.

CHAKCHOUKA

Ingredients

- Onions - 2, finely chopped.
- Green bell peppers - 2, chopped.
- Tomatoes - 5, peeled and chopped.
- Garlic cloves - 2, minced.
- Olive oil - 3 tablespoons.
- Paprika - 1 teaspoon.
- Cumin - 1/2 teaspoon.
- Eggs - 4.
- Salt and pepper - to taste.

Instructions

1. Heat olive oil in a large pan and sauté onions and bell peppers until soft.

2. Add garlic, tomatoes, paprika, and cumin. Cook until the mixture has thickened.

3. Make four wells in the mixture and crack an egg into each. Cover and cook until the eggs are set to your liking.

4. Season with salt and pepper, and serve hot.

TUNISIAN FALAFEL

Ingredients

- Chickpeas - 2 cups, soaked overnight and drained.
- Onion - 1, chopped.
- Garlic cloves - 3, minced.
- Fresh parsley - 1/2 cup, chopped.
- Fresh cilantro - 1/2 cup, chopped.
- Ground cumin - 1 teaspoon.
- Ground coriander - 1 teaspoon.
- Salt and pepper - to taste.
- Baking powder - 1/2 teaspoon.
- Oil - for frying.

Instructions

1. Process the chickpeas, onion, garlic, parsley, cilantro, cumin, coriander, salt, and pepper in a food processor until well combined but not pureed.

2. Stir in baking powder.

3. Form the mixture into small balls and flatten slightly.

4. Heat oil in a deep fryer or large pan to 180°C (356°F) and fry the falafel in batches until golden brown.

5. Drain on paper towels and serve hot with tahini sauce or inside pita bread with vegetables.

OJJA (WITH MERGUEZ)

Ingredients

- Merguez sausages - 6.
- Onion - 1, finely chopped.
- Garlic cloves - 2, minced.
- Tomatoes - 4, chopped.
- Green bell pepper - 1, chopped.
- Tomato paste - 1 tablespoon.
- Harissa - 1 teaspoon, adjusted to taste.
- Eggs - 4.
- Olive oil - 2 tablespoons.
- Salt and pepper - to taste.
- Ground caraway - 1/2 teaspoon.
- Ground coriander - 1/2 teaspoon.

Instructions

1. In a skillet, heat olive oil over medium heat and cook the merguez sausages until browned. Remove and set aside.

2. In the same skillet, add onion, garlic, and bell pepper. Cook until soft.

3. Stir in chopped tomatoes, tomato paste, harissa, caraway, and coriander. Cook until the tomatoes break down into a sauce.

4. Slice the cooked merguez and add back to the skillet. Season with salt and pepper.

5. Make wells in the sauce and crack an egg into each. Cover and cook until the eggs are set to your liking.

6. Serve hot, directly from the skillet.

SALADS

Tunisian salads stand out for their distinctive attributes, setting them apart from other culinary elements in the region. These dishes are celebrated for their rich nutritional profile, offering a plethora of vitamins and minerals essential for a balanced diet. The versatility of Tunisian salads is notable, as they seamlessly incorporate a variety of fresh produce, grains, and spices, showcasing the country's agricultural diversity and culinary innovation.

The role of salads in Tunisian cuisine is pivotal, not only in terms of health benefits but also as a cultural expression. They are a testament to the art of combining simple ingredients to create flavors that are both complex and refreshing. This aspect of Tunisian salads underscores their importance in promoting a healthy lifestyle, with their low-calorie profiles and high nutrient density supporting overall wellness.

Tunisian salads are indispensable in a health-conscious diet, offering a harmonious blend of taste and nourishment. Their integral position in Tunisian cuisine highlights the tradition's commitment to meals that are both delightful and beneficial to health.

SALAD TUNISIENNE

Ingredients

- Lettuce - 1 head, chopped.
- Tomatoes - 2, diced.
- Cucumber - 1, sliced.
- Onion - 1 small, finely chopped.
- Hard-boiled eggs - 2, quartered.

- Tuna - 1 can, drained.
- Olives - a handful.
- Extra virgin olive oil - 3 tablespoons.
- Lemon juice - 1 tablespoon.
- Salt and pepper - to taste.

Instructions

1. In a large salad bowl, combine the lettuce, tomatoes, cucumber, and onion.

2. Top the salad with hard-boiled eggs, tuna, and olives.

3. Drizzle with extra virgin olive oil and lemon juice, then season with salt and pepper.

4. Toss gently to combine before serving.

CARROT SALAD WITH CUMIN

Ingredients

- Carrots - 4, grated.
- Garlic cloves - 2, minced.
- Cumin seeds - 1 teaspoon, toasted and ground.
- Extra virgin olive oil - 2 tablespoons.
- Lemon juice - 2 tablespoons.
- Fresh coriander - 2 tablespoons, chopped.
- Salt and pepper - to taste.

Instructions

1. In a large bowl, mix the grated carrots with the minced garlic and ground cumin.

2. Add the extra virgin olive oil and lemon juice, then season with salt and pepper.

3. Toss well to combine.

4. Garnish with fresh coriander before serving.

BEETROOT SALAD

Ingredients

- Beetroots - 3, cooked and diced.
- Garlic cloves - 2, minced.
- Extra virgin olive oil - 2 tablespoons.
- White vinegar - 1 tablespoon.
- Fresh parsley - 2 tablespoons, chopped.
- Salt and pepper - to taste.

Instructions

1. In a salad bowl, combine the diced beetroots with the minced garlic.

2. Dress with extra virgin olive oil and white vinegar, then season with salt and pepper.

3. Toss well to ensure all the beetroots are coated.

4. Sprinkle with chopped parsley before serving.

TUNA AND EGG SALAD

Ingredients

- Canned tuna - 1 can, drained.
- Hard-boiled eggs - 4, chopped.
- Mayonnaise - 3 tablespoons.
- Mustard - 1 teaspoon.
- Green onions - 2, chopped.
- Salt and pepper - to taste.

Instructions

1. In a mixing bowl, combine the drained tuna and chopped hard-boiled eggs.

2. Stir in mayonnaise and mustard until well mixed.

3. Add the chopped green onions, then season with salt and pepper to taste.

4. Mix gently until all ingredients are evenly distributed.

5. Refrigerate for at least 30 minutes before serving to allow flavors to meld.

CUCUMBER AND YOGURT SALAD

Ingredients

- Cucumber - 1 large, diced.
- Plain yogurt - 1 cup.
- Garlic cloves - 1, minced.
- Mint leaves - 2 tablespoons, chopped.
- Salt - 1/2 teaspoon.
- Olive oil - 1 tablespoon (optional).

Instructions

1. In a salad bowl, combine the diced cucumber with the plain yogurt and minced garlic.

2. Add the chopped mint leaves and salt, then mix well.

3. Drizzle with olive oil if using, and give it one last mix.

4. Chill in the refrigerator for about 20 minutes before serving.

ORANGE AND OLIVE SALAD

Ingredients

- Oranges - 4, peeled and sliced.
- Black olives - 1/2 cup, pitted.
- Red onion - 1 small, thinly sliced.
- Olive oil - 2 tablespoons.
- Lemon juice - 1 tablespoon.
- Salt - 1/4 teaspoon.
- Black pepper - 1/8 teaspoon.
- Fresh parsley - 2 tablespoons, chopped.

Instructions

1. Arrange the orange slices on a serving plate.

2. Sprinkle the black olives and red onion slices over the oranges.

3. In a small bowl, whisk together the olive oil, lemon juice, salt, and black pepper.

4. Drizzle the dressing over the salad.

5. Garnish with chopped parsley before serving.

GRILLED VEGETABLE SALAD

Ingredients

- Zucchini - 2, sliced lengthwise.
- Red bell peppers - 2, quartered.
- Eggplant - 1, sliced.
- Cherry tomatoes - 1 cup.
- Olive oil - 3 tablespoons.
- Balsamic vinegar - 1 tablespoon.

- Salt and pepper - to taste.
- Fresh basil - 1/4 cup, torn.

Instructions

1. Preheat the grill to medium-high heat.

2. Brush the vegetables with olive oil and season with salt and pepper.

3. Grill the vegetables until tender and slightly charred, about 3-4 minutes per side.

4. Arrange the grilled vegetables on a serving platter.

5. Drizzle with balsamic vinegar and sprinkle with fresh basil.

6. Serve warm or at room temperature.

POTATO AND OLIVE SALAD

Ingredients

- Potatoes - 4 medium, boiled and cubed.
- Black olives - 1/2 cup, sliced.
- Green olives - 1/2 cup, sliced.
- Olive oil - 3 tablespoons.
- Lemon juice - 2 tablespoons.
- Garlic - 1 clove, minced.
- Salt and pepper - to taste.
- Fresh parsley - 1/4 cup, chopped.

Instructions

1. In a large bowl, combine the boiled and cubed potatoes with the black and green olives.

2. In a small bowl, whisk together the olive oil, lemon juice, minced garlic, salt, and pepper.

3. Pour the dressing over the potato and olive mixture and toss to coat evenly.

4. Garnish with chopped parsley before serving.

CABBAGE SALAD

Ingredients

- Green cabbage - 1/2 head, finely shredded.
- Carrots - 2, grated.
- Green apples - 1, thinly sliced.
- Lemon juice - 2 tablespoons.
- Olive oil - 2 tablespoons.
- Mustard - 1 teaspoon.
- Honey - 1 teaspoon.
- Salt and pepper - to taste.
- Fresh mint - 1/4 cup, chopped.

Instructions

1. In a large salad bowl, combine the shredded cabbage, grated carrots, and thinly sliced apples.

2. In a small bowl, whisk together the lemon juice, olive oil, mustard, honey, salt, and pepper to create the dressing.

3. Pour the dressing over the salad and toss well to coat.

4. Garnish with chopped mint before serving.

FATTOUSH TUNISIAN STYLE

Ingredients

- Romaine lettuce - 1 head, chopped.
- Cucumbers - 2, diced.
- Tomatoes - 3, diced.
- Radishes - 6, thinly sliced.
- Green onions - 3, chopped.
- Stale bread - 2 cups, cubed and toasted.
- Extra virgin olive oil - 1/4 cup.
- Lemon juice - 3 tablespoons.
- Sumac - 1 teaspoon.
- Salt and pepper - to taste.
- Fresh mint - 1/4 cup, chopped.
- Fresh parsley - 1/4 cup, chopped.

Instructions

1. In a large salad bowl, combine the chopped lettuce, diced cucumbers, diced tomatoes, thinly sliced radishes, and chopped green onions.

2. Add the cubed and toasted stale bread to the salad.

3. In a small bowl, whisk together the extra virgin olive oil, lemon juice, sumac, salt, and pepper to create the dressing.

4. Pour the dressing over the salad and toss well to coat all the ingredients evenly.

5. Garnish with chopped mint and parsley before serving.

EGGPLANT SALAD

Ingredients

- Eggplants - 3, large.
- Garlic cloves - 2, minced.
- Lemon juice - 2 tablespoons.
- Olive oil - 3 tablespoons.
- Salt and pepper - to taste.
- Fresh parsley - 1/4 cup, chopped.

Instructions

1. Prick the eggplants with a fork and grill over medium heat until the skin is charred and the flesh is soft.

2. Peel the charred skin off the eggplants and mash the flesh with a fork.

3. Mix the mashed eggplant with minced garlic, lemon juice, olive oil, salt, and pepper.

4. Garnish with chopped fresh parsley before serving.

ARTICHOKE SALAD

Ingredients

- Artichoke hearts - 6, cooked and quartered.
- Olives - 1/4 cup, sliced.
- Red onion - 1 small, thinly sliced.
- Extra virgin olive oil - 2 tablespoons.
- Lemon juice - 1 tablespoon.
- Salt and pepper - to taste.
- Fresh parsley - 2 tablespoons, chopped.

Instructions

1. Combine the artichoke hearts, sliced olives, and thinly sliced red onion in a salad bowl.

2. Drizzle with extra virgin olive oil and lemon juice, then season with salt and pepper.

3. Toss gently to combine all the ingredients.

4. Sprinkle with chopped fresh parsley before serving.

SLICED TOMATO AND ONION SALAD

Ingredients

- Tomatoes - 4, large, sliced.
- Red onion - 1 medium, thinly sliced.
- Olive oil - 3 tablespoons.
- Vinegar - 1 tablespoon.
- Salt and pepper - to taste.
- Fresh mint - 2 tablespoons, chopped.

Instructions

1. Arrange the sliced tomatoes and thinly sliced red onion on a serving platter.

2. Drizzle with olive oil and vinegar, then season with salt and pepper.

3. Garnish with chopped fresh mint before serving.

RADISH AND MINT SALAD

Ingredients

- Radishes - 1 bunch, thinly sliced.
- Mint leaves - 1/4 cup, chopped.
- Lemon juice - 2 tablespoons.
- Olive oil - 2 tablespoons.
- Salt and pepper - to taste.

Instructions

1. Combine the thinly sliced radishes and chopped mint leaves in a salad bowl.

2. Dress with lemon juice and olive oil, then season with salt and pepper.

3. Toss well to combine before serving.

SPICY CARROT AND CHICKPEA SALAD

Ingredients

- Carrots - 4, grated.
- Chickpeas - 1 can (400g), drained and rinsed.
- Garlic cloves - 2, minced.
- Harissa - 1 tablespoon.
- Olive oil - 3 tablespoons.
- Lemon juice - 2 tablespoons.
- Cumin - 1 teaspoon.
- Salt and pepper - to taste.
- Fresh cilantro - 1/4 cup, chopped.

Instructions

1. In a large bowl, mix the grated carrots and chickpeas.

2. In a small bowl, whisk together the minced garlic, harissa, olive oil, lemon juice, cumin, salt, and pepper to make the dressing.

3. Pour the dressing over the carrot and chickpea mixture and toss well to coat.

4. Garnish with chopped fresh cilantro before serving.

SOUPS

Tunisian soups are distinguished by their unique characteristics, which set them apart from other culinary components within the country's gastronomy. Rich in essential nutrients, these soups offer a blend of flavors and health benefits, leveraging the bountiful local produce and spices. Their adaptability is remarkable, allowing for the creation of both hearty and light dishes that reflect Tunisia's seasonal ingredients and culinary heritage.

In the context of Tunisian cuisine, soups play a crucial role beyond mere sustenance; they embody the culinary tradition's dedication to wellness and flavor. These soups, often a melange of vegetables, legumes, and sometimes meats, are a testament to the ingenuity in maximizing taste while promoting a healthful diet. This fusion of ingredients not only nourishes the body but also provides a comforting warmth and complexity that is deeply rooted in Tunisian culture.

Serving as a cornerstone of healthy eating, Tunisian soups are essential for those seeking a diet that balances nutrition with gastronomic pleasure. Their prominence in the Tunisian diet underscores a commitment to meals that support well-being without sacrificing taste.

CHORBA FRIK

Ingredients

- Lamb meat - 500 grams, cubed.
- Onion - 1, finely chopped.
- Tomatoes - 2, grated.
- Frik (cracked wheat) - 1 cup.

- Chickpeas - 1 cup, soaked overnight and drained.
- Carrot - 1, diced.
- Celery stalk - 1, chopped.
- Fresh coriander - 1/4 cup, chopped.
- Paprika - 1 teaspoon.
- Cumin - 1/2 teaspoon.
- Salt and pepper - to taste.
- Olive oil - 2 tablespoons.
- Water - 2 liters.

Instructions

1. In a large pot, heat the olive oil over medium heat and sauté the onion until translucent.

2. Add the lamb cubes and brown on all sides.

3. Stir in the grated tomatoes, chickpeas, carrot, celery, and spices. Cook for 5 minutes.

4. Add the water and bring to a boil. Reduce heat, cover, and simmer for 30 minutes.

5. Add the frik and continue to simmer for another 30 minutes, or until the soup thickens and the meat is tender.

6. Adjust the seasoning, stir in the fresh coriander, and serve hot.

LABLABI (CHICKPEA SOUP)

Ingredients

- Chickpeas - 2 cups, soaked overnight and drained.
- Garlic cloves - 4, minced.
- Ground cumin - 1 teaspoon.

- Harissa paste - 1 tablespoon.
- Olive oil - 2 tablespoons.
- Lemon juice - from 1 lemon.
- Salt and pepper - to taste.
- Bread - 2 slices, torn into small pieces.
- Water - 2 liters.

Instructions

1. In a large pot, combine the chickpeas and water. Bring to a boil, then reduce heat and simmer until chickpeas are tender, about 1 hour.

2. In a small skillet, heat the olive oil and sauté the garlic until fragrant. Add the cumin and harissa, stirring for 1 minute.

3. Add the garlic-spice mixture to the chickpeas. Season with salt and pepper.

4. Stir in the lemon juice and torn bread pieces. Cook for an additional 10 minutes.

5. Serve hot, garnished with additional lemon slices if desired.

HARIRA

Ingredients

- Lamb meat - 300 grams, cubed.
- Onion - 1, chopped.
- Lentils - 1/2 cup, rinsed.
- Chickpeas - 1/2 cup, soaked overnight and drained.
- Tomato paste - 2 tablespoons.
- Fresh cilantro - 1/4 cup, chopped.

- Fresh parsley - 1/4 cup, chopped.
- Rice - 1/4 cup.
- Paprika - 1 teaspoon.
- Cinnamon - 1/2 teaspoon.
- Ginger powder - 1/2 teaspoon.
- Salt and pepper - to taste.
- Water - 2.5 liters.

Instructions

1. In a large pot, cook the lamb, onion, and spices with a little oil until the meat is browned.

2. Add the lentils, chickpeas, tomato paste, and water. Bring to a boil, then reduce heat and simmer for 45 minutes.

3. Add the rice, cilantro, and parsley. Continue to simmer for another 30 minutes, or until the rice and lentils are cooked through.

4. Adjust the seasoning and serve hot.

BISSARA (FAVA BEAN SOUP)

Ingredients

- Dried fava beans - 2 cups, peeled and soaked overnight.
- Garlic cloves - 3, minced.
- Ground cumin - 1 teaspoon.
- Olive oil - 3 tablespoons.
- Lemon juice - 1 tablespoon.
- Salt and pepper - to taste.
- Water - 2 liters.

Instructions

1. Drain the soaked fava beans and place them in a large pot with water. Bring to a boil and then simmer for 1-2 hours, or until the beans are very soft.

2. Once the beans are cooked, blend the mixture using an immersion blender until smooth.

3. Add the minced garlic, cumin, olive oil, and lemon juice. Season with salt and pepper.

4. Cook for an additional 10 minutes, stirring frequently.

5. Serve hot, drizzled with olive oil if desired.

LENTIL SOUP

Ingredients

- Red lentils - 1 cup, rinsed.
- Carrot - 1, diced.
- Onion - 1, chopped.
- Garlic cloves - 2, minced.
- Tomato paste - 2 tablespoons.
- Cumin - 1 teaspoon.
- Vegetable broth - 4 cups.
- Olive oil - 2 tablespoons.
- Salt and pepper - to taste.
- Lemon wedges - for serving.

Instructions

1. In a large pot, heat the olive oil over medium heat. Add the onions, carrots, and garlic. Cook until the vegetables are soft.

2. Stir in the tomato paste, cumin, and rinsed lentils.

3. Add the vegetable broth and bring to a boil. Reduce heat to low and simmer for 20-25 minutes, or until the lentils are fully cooked.

4. Season with salt and pepper to taste.

5. Serve hot with lemon wedges on the side.

PUMPKIN SOUP WITH HARISSA

Ingredients

- Pumpkin - 1 kg, peeled and cubed.
- Onion - 1, chopped.
- Garlic cloves - 2, minced.
- Chicken or vegetable broth - 4 cups.
- Harissa paste - 1 tablespoon, adjust to taste.
- Heavy cream - 1/2 cup.
- Olive oil - 2 tablespoons.
- Salt and pepper - to taste.
- Fresh cilantro - for garnish.

Instructions

1. In a large pot, heat olive oil over medium heat and sauté the onion and garlic until soft.

2. Add the pumpkin cubes and cook for a few minutes until slightly softened.

3. Pour in the broth and bring to a boil. Lower the heat and simmer until the pumpkin is completely soft.

4. Use an immersion blender to puree the soup until smooth.

5. Stir in the harissa paste and heavy cream, and season with salt and pepper.

6. Serve hot, garnished with fresh cilantro.

BARLEY SOUP

Ingredients

- Pearl barley - 1 cup, rinsed.
- Carrots - 2, diced.
- Onion - 1, chopped.
- Celery stalks - 2, chopped.
- Chicken or vegetable broth - 6 cups.
- Olive oil - 1 tablespoon.
- Bay leaves - 2.
- Salt and pepper - to taste.

Instructions

1. In a large pot, heat olive oil over medium heat. Add the onions, carrots, and celery and sauté until the vegetables are softened.

2. Add the rinsed barley, broth, and bay leaves. Bring to a boil.

3. Reduce heat to low, cover, and simmer for about 1 hour or until the barley is tender.

4. Season with salt and pepper to taste.

5. Remove bay leaves before serving.

FISH SOUP

Ingredients

- Fish fillets - 500 grams, diced.
- Onion - 1, chopped.
- Garlic cloves - 2, minced.
- Tomatoes - 2, chopped.
- Potato - 1, diced.
- Fish or vegetable broth - 4 cups.
- Olive oil - 2 tablespoons.
- Saffron - a pinch.
- Salt and pepper - to taste.
- Lemon juice - 1 tablespoon.
- Fresh parsley - for garnish.

Instructions

1. In a large pot, heat olive oil over medium heat and sauté the onion and garlic until soft.

2. Add the tomatoes and potato, cook for a few minutes.

3. Pour in the broth and bring to a boil. Add the saffron.

4. Reduce heat to simmer and add the fish. Cook until the fish is cooked through and the potatoes are tender.

5. Season with salt, pepper, and lemon juice.

6. Serve hot, garnished with fresh parsley.

TOMATO AND BREAD SOUP

Ingredients

- Ripe tomatoes - 6, chopped.

- Stale bread - 200 grams, torn into pieces.
- Onion - 1, chopped.
- Garlic cloves - 2, minced.
- Chicken or vegetable broth - 4 cups.
- Olive oil - 3 tablespoons.
- Sugar - 1 teaspoon (optional).
- Salt and pepper - to taste.
- Fresh basil - for garnish.

Instructions

1. In a large pot, heat olive oil over medium heat. Add the onions and garlic, and sauté until soft.

2. Add the chopped tomatoes and cook for a few minutes until they begin to break down.

3. Add the broth and bring to a boil. Reduce heat and simmer for 15 minutes.

4. Add the torn bread pieces and simmer until the bread is completely soaked and the soup thickens.

5. Season with sugar (if using), salt, and pepper.

6. Serve hot, garnished with fresh basil.

MEATBALL AND VEGETABLE SOUP

Ingredients

- Ground beef - 500 grams.
- Breadcrumbs - 1/2 cup.
- Egg - 1.
- Carrots - 2, diced.
- Zucchini - 2, diced.
- Onion - 1, chopped.

- Garlic cloves - 2, minced.
- Tomato paste - 2 tablespoons.
- Chicken or beef broth - 6 cups.
- Olive oil - 1 tablespoon.
- Salt and pepper - to taste.
- Fresh parsley - for garnish.

Instructions

1. In a bowl, mix ground beef, breadcrumbs, and egg. Season with salt and pepper, and form into small meatballs.

2. In a large pot, heat olive oil over medium heat. Add the onions and garlic, and sauté until soft.

3. Add the carrots, zucchini, and tomato paste. Cook for a few minutes.

4. Pour in the broth and bring to a boil. Add the meatballs.

5. Reduce heat to simmer and cook until the meatballs are cooked through and the vegetables are tender.

6. Season with salt and pepper to taste.

7. Serve hot, garnished with fresh parsley.

CHICKEN AND RICE SOUP

Ingredients

- Chicken breasts - 2, boneless and skinless.
- Rice - 1 cup.
- Carrots - 2, diced.
- Celery stalks - 2, diced.

- Onion - 1, diced.
- Chicken broth - 6 cups.
- Olive oil - 2 tablespoons.
- Salt and pepper - to taste.
- Fresh parsley - 1/4 cup, chopped.

Instructions

1. In a large pot, heat olive oil over medium heat. Add the onion, carrots, and celery, and sauté until softened.

2. Add the chicken breasts and chicken broth. Bring to a boil, then reduce heat and simmer until the chicken is cooked through.

3. Remove the chicken from the pot, shred it, and return it to the pot.

4. Add the rice, salt, and pepper. Simmer until the rice is tender.

5. Serve hot, garnished with fresh parsley.

SEAFOOD BISQUE

Ingredients

- Mixed seafood - 500 grams (shrimp, scallops, and crab meat).
- Butter - 2 tablespoons.
- Onion - 1, finely chopped.
- Garlic cloves - 2, minced.
- Tomato paste - 1 tablespoon.
- Fish stock - 4 cups.
- Heavy cream - 1 cup.
- Dry white wine - 1/2 cup.
- Bay leaf - 1.

- Thyme - 1 teaspoon, dried.
- Salt and pepper - to taste.

Instructions

1. In a large pot, melt butter over medium heat. Add the onion and garlic, and cook until soft.

2. Stir in the tomato paste and cook for 1 minute.

3. Add the fish stock, heavy cream, white wine, bay leaf, and thyme. Bring to a simmer.

4. Add the mixed seafood, and cook until just done.

5. Season with salt and pepper to taste. Serve hot, with crusty bread if desired.

SPINACH AND LENTIL SOUP

Ingredients

- Green lentils - 1 cup, rinsed.
- Spinach - 2 cups, chopped.
- Carrots - 2, diced.
- Onion - 1, diced.
- Garlic cloves - 2, minced.
- Vegetable broth - 6 cups.
- Olive oil - 2 tablespoons.
- Cumin - 1 teaspoon.
- Salt and pepper - to taste.

Instructions

1. In a large pot, heat olive oil over medium heat. Add the onion, carrots, and garlic, and cook until the vegetables start to soften.

2. Add the lentils, vegetable broth, and cumin. Bring to a boil, then reduce heat and simmer until the lentils are tender.

3. Add the chopped spinach and cook until wilted.

4. Season with salt and pepper to taste.

5. Serve hot.

SORGHUM SOUP

Ingredients

- Sorghum grains - 1 cup, rinsed.
- Tomatoes - 2, diced.
- Onion - 1, diced.
- Garlic cloves - 2, minced.
- Carrot - 1, diced.
- Vegetable broth - 6 cups.
- Olive oil - 2 tablespoons.
- Cumin - 1 teaspoon.
- Paprika - 1 teaspoon.
- Salt and pepper - to taste.

Instructions

1. In a large pot, heat olive oil over medium heat. Add the onion, garlic, and carrots, and cook until softened.

2. Add the sorghum grains, diced tomatoes, vegetable broth, cumin, and paprika. Bring to a boil.

3. Reduce heat to low and simmer, covered, until the sorghum is tender, about 1 hour.

4. Season with salt and pepper to taste.

5. Serve hot, garnished with fresh herbs if desired.

CARROT AND CORIANDER SOUP

Ingredients

- Carrots - 500 grams, peeled and diced.
- Potato - 1 large, peeled and diced.
- Onion - 1, chopped.
- Ground coriander - 1 teaspoon.
- Fresh coriander - 1/4 cup, chopped.
- Vegetable broth - 4 cups.
- Olive oil - 2 tablespoons.
- Salt and pepper - to taste.

Instructions

1. In a large pot, heat olive oil over medium heat. Add the onion and cook until soft.

2. Add the carrots, potato, and ground coriander. Cook for a few minutes, stirring occasionally.

3. Pour in the vegetable broth and bring to a boil. Reduce heat and simmer until the vegetables are tender.

4. Use an immersion blender to puree the soup until smooth.

5. Stir in the fresh coriander, and season with salt and pepper to taste.

6. Serve hot.

STEWS

Tunisian stews are celebrated for their distinct characteristics, distinguishing them sharply from other components of the nation's culinary landscape. They are nutritionally dense, incorporating a wide array of vegetables, legumes, and meats, all simmered to perfection to unlock deep, complex flavors. The versatility of these stews is evident in their ability to blend traditional spices and ingredients, creating dishes that are both comforting and invigorating.

The significance of stews in Tunisian cuisine cannot be overstated, serving not just as a source of sustenance but as a cultural emblem of hospitality and warmth. They marry the richness of Tunisian agriculture with culinary creativity, resulting in meals that are hearty, healthful, and steeped in tradition. This culinary practice underscores the importance of a balanced diet, utilizing locally sourced ingredients to offer dishes that are both nourishing and satisfying.

Tunisian stews are pivotal for anyone looking to embrace a diet that is as flavorful as it is beneficial for health. Their integral role in the cuisine highlights a dedication to crafting dishes that delight the palate while fostering well-being.

MARQA (TUNISIAN STEW)

Ingredients

- Lamb - 500 grams, cubed.
- Onions - 2, finely chopped.
- Tomato paste - 2 tablespoons.
- Potatoes - 3, cubed.

- Carrots - 2, sliced.
- Zucchini - 2, sliced.
- Chickpeas - 1 cup, soaked overnight and drained.
- Harissa - 1 tablespoon.
- Ground coriander - 1 teaspoon.
- Ground caraway - 1 teaspoon.
- Olive oil - 3 tablespoons.
- Salt and pepper - to taste.
- Water - enough to cover the ingredients.

Instructions

1. In a large pot, heat the olive oil over medium heat. Add the onions and sauté until they become translucent.

2. Add the lamb cubes and brown on all sides.

3. Stir in the tomato paste, harissa, ground coriander, and ground caraway. Cook for a few minutes, stirring constantly.

4. Add the potatoes, carrots, zucchini, and chickpeas to the pot. Season with salt and pepper.

5. Cover the ingredients with water and bring to a boil. Reduce the heat and simmer until the meat is tender and the vegetables are cooked through, about 1 hour.

6. Serve hot with Tunisian bread or over couscous.

OJJA WITH SEAFOOD

Ingredients

- Shrimp - 200 grams, peeled and deveined.
- Squid - 200 grams, sliced into rings.
- Tomatoes - 3, chopped.

- Garlic cloves - 2, minced.
- Harissa - 1 tablespoon, adjusted to taste.
- Eggs - 4.
- Olive oil - 2 tablespoons.
- Cumin - 1 teaspoon.
- Salt and pepper - to taste.
- Fresh parsley - for garnish.

Instructions

1. In a large skillet, heat the olive oil over medium heat. Add the garlic and sauté until fragrant.

2. Add the chopped tomatoes and harissa. Cook until the tomatoes break down into a sauce.

3. Stir in the shrimp and squid. Season with cumin, salt, and pepper. Cook until the seafood is just done.

4. Crack the eggs over the sauce. Cover and cook until the eggs are set to your liking.

5. Garnish with fresh parsley before serving.

LAMB AND VEGETABLE TAGINE

Ingredients

- Lamb shoulder - 800 grams, cut into chunks.
- Onions - 2, sliced.
- Garlic cloves - 3, minced.
- Carrots - 3, cut into chunks.
- Potatoes - 3, cut into chunks.
- Zucchini - 2, cut into chunks.
- Tomato paste - 2 tablespoons.
- Chicken broth - 2 cups.
- Ras el hanout - 2 teaspoons.

- Cinnamon stick - 1.
- Prunes - 1 cup.
- Almonds - 1/2 cup, toasted.
- Olive oil - 3 tablespoons.
- Salt and pepper - to taste.
- Fresh cilantro - for garnish.

Instructions

1. In a tagine or large pot, heat the olive oil over medium heat. Add the lamb and brown on all sides. Remove and set aside.

2. In the same pot, add the onions and garlic. Sauté until soft.

3. Return the lamb to the pot. Stir in the tomato paste, chicken broth, ras el hanout, and cinnamon stick. Bring to a boil, then reduce heat, cover, and simmer for 1 hour.

4. Add the carrots, potatoes, and zucchini. Continue to cook until the vegetables are tender, about 30 minutes.

5. Stir in the prunes and cook for an additional 10 minutes.

6. Garnish with toasted almonds and fresh cilantro before serving.

CHICKEN AND CHICKPEA STEW

Ingredients

- Chicken thighs - 4, bone-in and skin-on.
- Chickpeas - 1 cup, soaked overnight and drained.
- Onion - 1, chopped.
- Garlic cloves - 2, minced.

- Tomatoes - 2, chopped.
- Chicken broth - 4 cups.
- Olive oil - 2 tablespoons.
- Turmeric - 1 teaspoon.
- Paprika - 1 teaspoon.
- Cumin - 1 teaspoon.
- Salt and pepper - to taste.
- Fresh coriander - 1/4 cup, chopped.

Instructions

1. In a large pot, heat the olive oil over medium heat. Add the chicken thighs and brown on both sides. Remove and set aside.

2. In the same pot, add the onion and garlic. Cook until soft.

3. Add the tomatoes, chickpeas, chicken broth, turmeric, paprika, and cumin. Season with salt and pepper.

4. Return the chicken to the pot. Cover and simmer until the chicken is cooked through and the chickpeas are tender, about 1 hour.

5. Garnish with fresh coriander before serving.

BEEF AND PRUNE STEW

Ingredients

- Beef - 500 grams, cubed.
- Prunes - 1 cup.
- Onions - 2, finely chopped.
- Garlic cloves - 2, minced.
- Beef broth - 4 cups.
- Cinnamon stick - 1.

- Ginger powder - 1 teaspoon.
- Saffron threads - a pinch.
- Olive oil - 2 tablespoons.
- Salt and pepper - to taste.
- Sesame seeds - for garnish.

Instructions

1. In a large pot, heat the olive oil over medium heat. Add the beef cubes and brown on all sides. Remove and set aside.

2. In the same pot, add the onions and garlic. Cook until soft.

3. Return the beef to the pot. Add the beef broth, cinnamon stick, ginger powder, and saffron. Season with salt and pepper.

4. Bring to a boil, then reduce heat, cover, and simmer for 1.5 hours, or until the beef is tender.

5. Add the prunes and continue to cook for 30 minutes, or until the prunes are soft.

6. Garnish with sesame seeds before serving.

FISH AND POTATO STEW

Ingredients

- White fish fillets - 500 grams, cut into chunks.
- Potatoes - 3, peeled and cubed.
- Onion - 1, finely chopped.
- Garlic cloves - 2, minced.
- Tomato paste - 2 tablespoons.
- Chicken or fish broth - 4 cups.

- Olive oil - 2 tablespoons.
- Paprika - 1 teaspoon.
- Cumin - 1/2 teaspoon.
- Salt and pepper - to taste.
- Fresh parsley - 1/4 cup, chopped for garnish.

Instructions

1. In a large pot, heat the olive oil over medium heat. Add the onion and garlic, and sauté until softened.

2. Stir in the tomato paste, paprika, and cumin. Cook for 1 minute, stirring constantly.

3. Add the potatoes and broth. Bring to a boil, then reduce heat and simmer until the potatoes are almost tender.

4. Add the fish chunks, season with salt and pepper, and simmer until the fish is cooked through.

5. Serve hot, garnished with fresh parsley.

SPINACH AND MEAT STEW

Ingredients

- Lamb or beef - 500 grams, cubed.
- Spinach - 400 grams, washed and chopped.
- Onion - 1, chopped.
- Garlic cloves - 3, minced.
- Chickpeas - 1 cup, soaked overnight and drained.
- Tomatoes - 2, diced.
- Chicken or beef broth - 4 cups.
- Coriander powder - 1 teaspoon.
- Cumin - 1 teaspoon.
- Salt and pepper - to taste.

- Olive oil - 2 tablespoons.

Instructions

1. In a large pot, heat the olive oil over medium heat. Add the cubed meat and brown on all sides.

2. Add the onion and garlic, and sauté until translucent.

3. Stir in the tomatoes, chickpeas, coriander, cumin, salt, and pepper. Cook for a few minutes.

4. Add the broth and bring to a boil. Reduce heat and simmer until the meat is almost tender, about 1 hour.

5. Add the chopped spinach and cook until wilted and the stew is thickened, about 15 minutes. Adjust seasoning and serve hot.

ARTICHOKE AND PEA STEW

Ingredients

- Artichoke hearts - 6, quartered.
- Fresh or frozen peas - 1 cup.
- Onion - 1, chopped.
- Garlic cloves - 2, minced.
- Chicken or vegetable broth - 3 cups.
- Olive oil - 2 tablespoons.
- Lemon juice - 1 tablespoon.
- Salt and pepper - to taste.
- Fresh parsley - 1/4 cup, chopped for garnish.

Instructions

1. In a pot, heat the olive oil over medium heat. Add the onion and garlic, and cook until soft.

2. Add the artichoke hearts, peas, and broth. Season with salt and pepper.

3. Bring to a simmer and cook until the vegetables are tender, about 20 minutes.

4. Stir in the lemon juice.

5. Serve hot, garnished with fresh parsley.

SQUID AND TOMATO STEW

Ingredients

- Squid - 500 grams, cleaned and cut into rings.
- Tomatoes - 4, peeled and chopped.
- Onion - 1, chopped.
- Garlic cloves - 2, minced.
- Red chili flakes - 1/2 teaspoon (optional).
- White wine - 1/2 cup.
- Olive oil - 2 tablespoons.
- Salt and pepper - to taste.
- Fresh parsley - 1/4 cup, chopped for garnish.

Instructions

1. In a large pot, heat the olive oil over medium heat. Add the onion, garlic, and red chili flakes, and cook until the onion is soft.

2. Add the squid and cook for a few minutes until it turns opaque.

3. Pour in the white wine and let it simmer until reduced by half.

4. Add the tomatoes and season with salt and pepper. Cover and simmer for about 30 minutes, or until the squid is tender.

5. Garnish with fresh parsley and serve hot.

PUMPKIN AND LAMB STEW

Ingredients

- Lamb - 500 grams, cubed.
- Pumpkin - 500 grams, peeled and cubed.
- Onion - 1, chopped.
- Garlic cloves - 2, minced.
- Ground cinnamon - 1/2 teaspoon.
- Ground ginger - 1/2 teaspoon.
- Chicken or beef broth - 4 cups.
- Tomato paste - 1 tablespoon.
- Olive oil - 2 tablespoons.
- Salt and pepper - to taste.
- Fresh cilantro - 1/4 cup, chopped for garnish.

Instructions

1. In a large pot, heat the olive oil over medium heat. Add the lamb cubes and brown on all sides. Remove and set aside.

2. In the same pot, add the onion and garlic, and cook until soft.

3. Return the lamb to the pot, along with the pumpkin, cinnamon, ginger, broth, and tomato paste. Season with salt and pepper.

4. Bring to a boil, then reduce the heat and simmer until the lamb and pumpkin are tender, about 1 hour.

5. Adjust seasoning and serve hot, garnished with fresh cilantro.

CHAKCHOUKA WITH MEAT

Ingredients

- Beef or lamb - 500 grams, cubed.
- Green bell peppers - 2, chopped.
- Tomatoes - 4, peeled and chopped.
- Onion - 1, chopped.
- Garlic cloves - 2, minced.
- Eggs - 4.
- Ground cumin - 1 teaspoon.
- Paprika - 1 teaspoon.
- Harissa paste - 1 tablespoon, optional.
- Olive oil - 3 tablespoons.
- Salt and pepper - to taste.
- Fresh parsley - for garnish.

Instructions

1. Heat the olive oil in a large skillet over medium heat. Add the onion and garlic, and sauté until soft.

2. Add the meat and cook until browned on all sides.

3. Stir in the bell peppers, tomatoes, cumin, paprika, and harissa paste (if using). Season with salt and pepper.

4. Cover and simmer over low heat until the meat is tender and the vegetables are cooked down, about 30-40 minutes.

5. Make four wells in the mixture and crack an egg into each. Cover and cook until the eggs are set to your liking.

6. Garnish with fresh parsley before serving.

EGGPLANT AND BEEF STEW

Ingredients

- Beef - 500 grams, cubed.
- Eggplants - 2, cubed and salted.
- Tomatoes - 3, chopped.
- Garlic cloves - 3, minced.
- Onion - 1, chopped.
- Tomato paste - 2 tablespoons.
- Beef broth - 4 cups.
- Olive oil - 2 tablespoons.
- Baharat spice mix - 1 teaspoon.
- Salt and pepper - to taste.

Instructions

1. Rinse the eggplant cubes to remove excess salt and pat dry.

2. In a large pot, heat the olive oil over medium heat. Add the onions and garlic, and sauté until softened.

3. Add the beef and brown on all sides.

4. Stir in the tomatoes, tomato paste, and baharat spice mix. Cook for a few minutes.

5. Add the eggplants and beef broth. Season with salt and pepper.

6. Bring to a boil, then reduce heat and simmer until the beef and eggplants are tender, about 1 hour.

7. Adjust seasoning and serve hot.

TUNISIAN RATATOUILLE

Ingredients

- Zucchini - 2, sliced.
- Eggplants - 2, cubed.
- Green bell peppers - 2, chopped.
- Tomatoes - 4, chopped.
- Onion - 1, chopped.
- Garlic cloves - 3, minced.
- Tomato paste - 1 tablespoon.
- Olive oil - 4 tablespoons.
- Harissa - 1 teaspoon, optional.
- Salt and pepper - to taste.
- Fresh coriander - 1/4 cup, chopped.

Instructions

1. In a large pot, heat the olive oil over medium heat. Add the onions and garlic, and cook until soft.

2. Add the green bell peppers, zucchini, and eggplants. Cook for a few minutes, stirring occasionally.

3. Stir in the tomatoes, tomato paste, and harissa (if using). Season with salt and pepper.

4. Cover and simmer over low heat until the vegetables are tender, about 20-30 minutes.

5. Adjust seasoning and garnish with fresh coriander before serving.

OKRA AND TOMATO STEW

Ingredients

- Okra - 500 grams, trimmed.
- Tomatoes - 4, peeled and chopped.
- Onion - 1, chopped.
- Garlic cloves - 2, minced.
- Lamb or beef - 300 grams, cubed.
- Tomato paste - 1 tablespoon.
- Beef broth - 3 cups.
- Olive oil - 2 tablespoons.
- Ground coriander - 1 teaspoon.
- Salt and pepper - to taste.

Instructions

1. In a large pot, heat the olive oil over medium heat. Add the onions, garlic, and meat. Brown the meat on all sides.

2. Add the tomatoes, tomato paste, ground coriander, and beef broth. Season with salt and pepper.

3. Bring to a boil, then reduce heat and simmer for 30 minutes.

4. Add the okra and continue to simmer until the okra is tender and the stew has thickened, about 20-30 minutes.

5. Adjust seasoning and serve hot.

MLOUKHIYA (JUTE LEAVES STEW)

Ingredients

- Dried mloukhiya (jute leaves) - 100 grams, finely ground.
- Lamb or beef - 500 grams, cubed.
- Garlic cloves - 6, minced.
- Onion - 1, chopped.
- Ground coriander - 2 teaspoons.
- Beef broth - 6 cups.
- Olive oil - 3 tablespoons.
- Baharat spice mix - 1 teaspoon.
- Salt and pepper - to taste.

Instructions

1. In a large pot, heat the olive oil over medium heat. Add the onions and garlic, and cook until the onions are translucent.

2. Add the cubed meat and brown on all sides.

3. Stir in the ground mloukhiya, ground coriander, and baharat spice mix. Mix well until the meat is coated with the spices and mloukhiya.

4. Pour in the beef broth and bring to a boil. Once boiling, reduce the heat to low, cover, and simmer for 2-3 hours, or until the meat is tender and the stew has thickened.

5. Season with salt and pepper to taste.

6. Serve hot, accompanied by Tunisian bread or over a bed of couscous.

SEAFOOD

Tunisian seafood is renowned for its distinctive qualities that set it apart from other elements of the nation's culinary offerings. Enriched by the Mediterranean's bounty, it boasts a high nutritional profile, abundant in omega-3 fatty acids, proteins, and vital minerals. The adaptability of seafood in Tunisian dishes is remarkable, allowing for an array of preparations from grilled to stewed, each highlighting the fresh, vibrant flavors of the sea.

This facet of Tunisian cuisine plays a vital role not only in providing sustenance but also in reflecting the country's long-standing relationship with the Mediterranean Sea. Seafood dishes are a testament to the culinary diversity of the region, incorporating a variety of spices and cooking techniques that enhance the natural flavors of the fish and shellfish. This culinary tradition emphasizes the importance of a diet rich in seafood, promoting health through dishes that are both delicious and nutritious.

Tunisian seafood is essential for those seeking a diet that combines the pleasures of gourmet flavors with the benefits of healthy eating. Its prominence in Tunisian cuisine underscores a commitment to meals that are as beneficial for the body as they are delightful to the palate.

GRILLED SARDINES

Ingredients

- Sardines - 1 kg, cleaned and gutted.
- Lemon juice - 2 tablespoons.
- Olive oil - 3 tablespoons.

- Garlic cloves - 2, minced.
- Paprika - 1 teaspoon.
- Cumin - 1/2 teaspoon.
- Salt and pepper - to taste.
- Fresh parsley - for garnish.

Instructions

1. In a small bowl, mix together lemon juice, olive oil, minced garlic, paprika, cumin, salt, and pepper.

2. Brush the sardines with the marinade and let them marinate for at least 30 minutes in the refrigerator.

3. Preheat the grill to medium-high heat.

4. Grill the sardines for 2-3 minutes on each side or until they are thoroughly cooked and charred slightly.

5. Serve hot, garnished with fresh parsley and lemon wedges on the side.

BAKED SEA BREAM WITH HARISSA

Ingredients

- Sea bream - 2 whole, cleaned and scaled.
- Harissa paste - 2 tablespoons.
- Olive oil - 4 tablespoons.
- Lemon - 1, sliced.
- Garlic cloves - 4, sliced.
- Salt and pepper - to taste.
- Fresh thyme - a few sprigs.

Instructions

1. Preheat the oven to 200°C (390°F).

2. Make a few slashes on each side of the sea bream.

3. Mix the harissa paste with 2 tablespoons of olive oil and rub it all over the fish, making sure to get some in the slashes and inside the cavity.

4. Season the inside of the fish with salt and pepper, and stuff with lemon slices, garlic slices, and thyme sprigs.

5. Drizzle the remaining olive oil over the fish and place on a baking tray.

6. Bake in the preheated oven for 20-25 minutes, or until the fish is cooked through and flakes easily.

7. Serve hot, garnished with more lemon slices and fresh herbs if desired.

TUNISIAN FISH TAGINE

Ingredients

- Fish fillets - 500 grams, firm white fish like cod or haddock.
- Potatoes - 3, thinly sliced.
- Tomatoes - 2, thinly sliced.
- Bell peppers - 2, sliced.
- Onion - 1, sliced.
- Garlic cloves - 2, minced.
- Harissa paste - 1 tablespoon, diluted in 1/4 cup water.
- Olive oil - 3 tablespoons.
- Lemon juice - 1 tablespoon.
- Cumin - 1 teaspoon.
- Coriander - 1 teaspoon, ground.
- Salt and pepper - to taste.
- Fresh cilantro - for garnish.

Instructions

1. Preheat your oven to 180°C (350°F).

2. In a tagine or oven-proof dish, layer the potatoes, tomatoes, bell peppers, and onion.

3. Mix the harissa paste with water, olive oil, lemon juice, cumin, coriander, salt, and pepper. Pour half of this mixture over the vegetables.

4. Place the fish fillets on top of the vegetables and pour the remaining harissa mixture over the fish.

5. Cover and bake in the preheated oven for 40-45 minutes, or until the vegetables are tender and the fish flakes easily. 6. Garnish with fresh cilantro before serving.

CALAMARI IN TOMATO SAUCE

Ingredients

- Calamari - 500 grams, cleaned and cut into rings.
- Tomato sauce - 2 cups.
- Garlic cloves - 2, minced.
- Olive oil - 2 tablespoons.
- White wine - 1/2 cup.
- Paprika - 1 teaspoon.
- Chili flakes - 1/2 teaspoon (optional).
- Salt and pepper - to taste.
- Parsley - 1/4 cup, chopped for garnish.

Instructions

1. Heat the olive oil in a skillet over medium heat. Add the

minced garlic and sauté until fragrant.

2. Add the calamari rings and cook for 2-3 minutes until they start to turn opaque.

3. Pour in the white wine and let it simmer until reduced by half.

4. Stir in the tomato sauce, paprika, and chili flakes (if using). Season with salt and pepper.

5. Simmer for 20-30 minutes, or until the sauce has thickened and the calamari is tender.

6. Serve hot, garnished with chopped parsley.

STUFFED MACKEREL

Ingredients

- Mackerel - 4 whole, cleaned and heads removed.
- Breadcrumbs - 1 cup.
- Onion - 1, finely chopped.
- Garlic cloves - 2, minced.
- Parsley - 1/4 cup, chopped.
- Lemon zest - from 1 lemon.
- Olive oil - 2 tablespoons, plus extra for drizzling.
- Salt and pepper - to taste.

Instructions

1. Preheat the oven to 200°C (390°F).

2. In a bowl, mix together the breadcrumbs, onion, garlic, parsley, lemon zest, olive oil, salt, and pepper to make the stuffing.

3. Stuff the cavity of each mackerel with the breadcrumb mixture.

4. Place the stuffed mackerel in a baking dish and drizzle with additional olive oil.

5. Bake in the preheated oven for 20-25 minutes, or until the fish is cooked through and the skin is crispy.

6. Serve hot, with lemon wedges and a side of your choice.

GRILLED SEA BASS

Ingredients

- Sea bass - 2 whole, cleaned and scaled.
- Olive oil - 4 tablespoons.
- Lemon - 2, sliced.
- Garlic cloves - 4, minced.
- Rosemary - 2 sprigs.
- Salt and pepper - to taste.

Instructions

1. Preheat the grill to medium-high heat.

2. Make several slashes on each side of the sea bass. Season the fish inside and out with salt and pepper.

3. Stuff the cavity of each fish with lemon slices, minced garlic, and rosemary sprigs.

4. Brush the outside of the fish with olive oil.

5. Grill the fish for about 7-10 minutes on each side, or until the skin is crispy and the flesh flakes easily with a

fork.

6. Serve hot, garnished with additional lemon slices and fresh herbs if desired.

SPICY FISH SOUP

Ingredients

- Firm white fish fillets - 500 grams, cubed.
- Onion - 1, chopped.
- Garlic cloves - 2, minced.
- Tomatoes - 3, diced.
- Potato - 1, cubed.
- Fish stock - 4 cups.
- Harissa - 1 tablespoon, or to taste.
- Cumin - 1 teaspoon.
- Coriander - 1 teaspoon.
- Olive oil - 2 tablespoons.
- Salt and pepper - to taste.
- Cilantro - 1/4 cup, chopped for garnish.

Instructions

1. In a large pot, heat the olive oil over medium heat. Add the onion and garlic, and cook until softened.

2. Add the tomatoes, potato, cumin, and coriander. Cook for a few minutes until the tomatoes start to break down.

3. Pour in the fish stock and bring to a simmer. Add the cubed fish and harissa. Season with salt and pepper.

4. Simmer for about 20 minutes, or until the fish is cooked through and the potatoes are tender.

5. Serve hot, garnished with chopped cilantro.

ANCHOVY AND EGG SALAD

Ingredients

- Anchovy fillets - 100 grams.
- Hard-boiled eggs - 4, quartered.
- Olives - 1/2 cup, sliced.
- Onion - 1 small, thinly sliced.
- Lettuce - 1 head, torn into bite-sized pieces.
- Olive oil - 3 tablespoons.
- Lemon juice - 2 tablespoons.
- Salt and pepper - to taste.

Instructions

1. In a large salad bowl, combine the lettuce, onion, olives, and anchovy fillets.

2. In a small bowl, whisk together the olive oil and lemon juice. Season with salt and pepper.

3. Pour the dressing over the salad and toss to coat.

4. Arrange the hard-boiled eggs on top of the salad.

5. Serve immediately.

MUSSELS IN SPICY BROTH

Ingredients

- Mussels - 1 kg, cleaned and debearded.
- Garlic cloves - 3, minced.
- Onion - 1, chopped.
- Tomato - 1, diced.
- White wine - 1 cup.
- Harissa - 2 teaspoons, or to taste.

- Olive oil - 2 tablespoons.
- Salt and pepper - to taste.
- Parsley - 1/4 cup, chopped for garnish.

Instructions

1. In a large pot, heat the olive oil over medium heat. Add the garlic and onion, and cook until softened.

2. Add the diced tomato and cook for a few minutes until it starts to break down.

3. Pour in the white wine and bring to a simmer. Stir in the harissa.

4. Add the mussels, cover the pot, and cook for 5-7 minutes, or until the mussels have opened. Discard any that remain closed.

5. Season with salt and pepper.

6. Serve the mussels and broth hot, garnished with chopped parsley.

TUNA STUFFED PEPPERS

Ingredients

- Bell peppers - 4, halved and deseeded.
- Tuna in oil - 2 cans, drained.
- Onion - 1 small, finely chopped.
- Garlic clove - 1, minced.
- Tomatoes - 2, diced.
- Capers - 2 tablespoons.
- Olive oil - 2 tablespoons, plus extra for drizzling.
- Salt and pepper - to taste.
- Breadcrumbs - 1/4 cup, for topping.

- Parsley - 2 tablespoons, chopped for garnish.

Instructions

1. Preheat the oven to 180°C (356°F).

2. In a bowl, mix together the tuna, onion, garlic, tomatoes, capers, olive oil, salt, and pepper.

3. Stuff each bell pepper half with the tuna mixture. Top with breadcrumbs and a drizzle of olive oil.

4. Place the stuffed peppers in a baking dish and bake for 25-30 minutes, or until the peppers are tender and the topping is golden brown.

5. Garnish with chopped parsley before serving.

SEAFOOD GRATIN

Ingredients

- Mixed seafood (shrimp, squid, mussels) - 500 grams.
- Bechamel sauce - 2 cups.
- Potatoes - 3, boiled and sliced.
- Onion - 1, finely chopped.
- Garlic cloves - 2, minced.
- Grated cheese - 1 cup.
- Breadcrumbs - 1/2 cup.
- Olive oil - 2 tablespoons.
- Salt and pepper - to taste.
- Parsley - 2 tablespoons, chopped for garnish.

Instructions

1. Preheat the oven to 200°C (390°F).

2. In a skillet, heat the olive oil over medium heat. Add the onion and garlic, and sauté until soft.

3. Add the mixed seafood and cook for about 5 minutes. Season with salt and pepper.

4. In a greased baking dish, layer the boiled and sliced potatoes.

5. Spread the cooked seafood over the potatoes.

6. Pour the bechamel sauce evenly over the seafood.

7. Sprinkle with grated cheese and breadcrumbs.

8. Bake in the preheated oven for 20-25 minutes, or until the top is golden and bubbly. Garnish with chopped parsley before serving.

FISH BALLS IN TOMATO SAUCE

Ingredients

- Fish fillets - 500 grams, minced.
- Breadcrumbs - 1/2 cup.
- Egg - 1.
- Onion - 1/2, finely chopped.
- Garlic clove - 1, minced.
- Cumin - 1 teaspoon.
- Paprika - 1 teaspoon.
- Salt and pepper - to taste.
- Tomato sauce - 2 cups.
- Olive oil - 2 tablespoons.

Instructions

1. In a bowl, combine the minced fish, breadcrumbs, egg,

onion, garlic, cumin, paprika, salt, and pepper. Mix well.

2. Form the mixture into small balls.

3. Heat the olive oil in a skillet over medium heat. Add the fish balls and cook until they are golden on all sides.

4. Pour the tomato sauce over the fish balls. Cover and simmer for 20 minutes.

5. Serve hot, garnished with fresh herbs if desired.

SEAFOOD OJJA

Ingredients

- Mixed seafood (shrimp, squid, mussels) - 500 grams.
- Tomatoes - 3, diced.
- Onion - 1, chopped.
- Garlic cloves - 2, minced.
- Harissa - 1 tablespoon, adjusted to taste.
- Eggs - 4.
- Olive oil - 3 tablespoons.
- Cumin - 1 teaspoon.
- Salt and pepper - to taste.
- Cilantro - 2 tablespoons, chopped for garnish.

Instructions

1. Heat the olive oil in a large skillet over medium heat. Add the onion and garlic, and cook until soft.

2. Add the tomatoes and harissa, and cook until the tomatoes have softened.

3. Add the mixed seafood and season with cumin, salt, and pepper. Cook for about 5 minutes, or until the seafood is nearly cooked through.

4. Make four wells in the mixture and crack an egg into each. Cover and cook until the eggs are set to your liking.

5. Garnish with cilantro before serving.

SQUID STUFFED WITH RICE

Ingredients

- Squid - 4 large, cleaned.
- Rice - 1 cup, cooked.
- Onion - 1, finely chopped.
- Pine nuts - 1/4 cup.
- Raisins - 1/4 cup.
- Parsley - 1/4 cup, chopped.
- Garlic cloves - 2, minced.
- Olive oil - 2 tablespoons.
- Salt and pepper - to taste.
- Lemon slices - for serving.

Instructions

1. Preheat the oven to 180°C (356°F).

2. In a skillet, heat 1 tablespoon of olive oil over medium heat. Sauté the onion, pine nuts, raisins, and garlic until the onion is translucent.

3. Mix the sautéed onion mixture with the cooked rice and chopped parsley. Season with salt and pepper.

4. Stuff each squid with the rice mixture, and close the openings with toothpicks.

5. Place the stuffed squid in a baking dish. Drizzle with the remaining olive oil.

6. Bake in the preheated oven for 20-25 minutes, or until the squid is tender. Serve hot with lemon slices on the side.

FRIED FISH WITH HARISSA SAUCE

Ingredients

- Fish fillets - 500 grams, any firm white fish.
- Flour - for dredging.
- Vegetable oil - for frying.
- Harissa paste - 2 tablespoons.
- Garlic clove - 1, minced.
- Olives - 1/2 cup, pitted and chopped.
- Lemon juice - 2 tablespoons.
- Olive oil - 1 tablespoon.
- Salt and pepper - to taste.

Instructions

1. Season the fish fillets with salt and pepper, then dredge in flour, shaking off any excess.

2. Heat the vegetable oil in a large skillet over medium-high heat. Fry the fish fillets until golden brown on both sides. Remove and drain on paper towels.

3. In a small bowl, mix together the harissa paste, minced garlic, chopped olives, lemon juice, and olive oil to make the sauce.

4. Serve the fried fish immediately, topped with the harissa sauce.

POULTRY

Tunisian poultry dishes stand out for their unique attributes, setting them apart from the broader spectrum of ingredients utilized in the country's cuisine. These dishes are particularly noted for their nutritional benefits, being rich sources of lean protein, essential vitamins, and minerals. Their versatility shines through in a variety of cooking methods, from roasting to stewing, each method infusing the poultry with the rich, aromatic spices that define Tunisian cuisine.

In Tunisian culinary tradition, poultry serves not merely as a source of nutrition but as a canvas for culinary artistry. The integration of poultry with a diverse range of spices and herbs exemplifies the creative synthesis of flavors, making these dishes a central component of the dining experience. This aspect of Tunisian cuisine highlights the balance between indulging the palate and maintaining a nutritious diet, with poultry dishes offering a hearty yet healthful option.

Poultry occupies a crucial place in the Tunisian diet, appealing to those seeking meals that are both flavorful and conducive to a healthy lifestyle. Its prominence within Tunisian cuisine showcases a dedication to providing meals that nourish as well as delight.

CHICKEN COUSCOUS

Ingredients

- Chicken thighs - 4, bone-in and skin-on.
- Couscous - 2 cups.
- Chicken broth - 4 cups.
- Carrots - 2, sliced.

- Zucchini - 2, sliced.
- Chickpeas - 1 cup, drained and rinsed.
- Onion - 1, chopped.
- Garlic cloves - 2, minced.
- Harissa paste - 1 tablespoon.
- Ground cumin - 1 teaspoon.
- Ground coriander - 1 teaspoon.
- Salt and pepper - to taste.
- Olive oil - 2 tablespoons.

Instructions

1. Preheat your oven to 200°C (390°F). Place the chicken thighs on a baking sheet, season with salt and pepper, and drizzle with olive oil. Roast for 25-30 minutes or until golden and cooked through.

2. Meanwhile, bring the chicken broth to a boil in a large pot. Add the couscous, cover, and remove from heat. Let it sit for 5 minutes, then fluff with a fork.

3. In another pot, heat 1 tablespoon of olive oil over medium heat. Sauté the onion and garlic until soft. Add the carrots, zucchini, chickpeas, harissa, cumin, and coriander. Cook until the vegetables are tender.

4. Mix the vegetable mixture into the couscous. Season with salt and pepper to taste.

5. Serve the couscous with the roasted chicken thighs on top.

ROASTED CHICKEN WITH PRESERVED LEMON

Ingredients

- Whole chicken - 1, about 1.5 kg.
- Preserved lemons - 2, sliced.
- Garlic cloves - 4, minced.
- Olives - 1 cup, green and pitted.
- Thyme - 1 tablespoon, fresh.
- Paprika - 1 teaspoon.
- Olive oil - 3 tablespoons.
- Salt and pepper - to taste.

Instructions

1. Preheat your oven to 220°C (428°F).

2. Rinse the chicken and pat dry with paper towels. Season the cavity with salt and pepper.

3. In a bowl, mix the preserved lemons, garlic, olives, thyme, and paprika with 1 tablespoon of olive oil. Stuff this mixture inside the chicken.

4. Rub the outside of the chicken with the remaining olive oil and season with salt and pepper.

5. Roast in the preheated oven for 1 hour or until the chicken is cooked through and the skin is crispy.

6. Serve hot, garnished with additional preserved lemon slices and olives if desired.

TUNISIAN CHICKEN TAGINE

Ingredients

- Chicken pieces - 500 grams.
- Onion - 1, finely chopped.
- Garlic cloves - 2, minced.
- Potatoes - 2, cubed.
- Carrots - 2, sliced.
- Tomato paste - 2 tablespoons.
- Chicken broth - 2 cups.
- Ras el hanout - 1 teaspoon.
- Chickpeas - 1 cup, cooked.
- Apricots - 1/2 cup, dried and chopped.
- Olive oil - 2 tablespoons.
- Salt and pepper - to taste.
- Cilantro - for garnish.

Instructions

1. Heat the olive oil in a tagine or heavy-bottomed pot over medium heat. Add the onion and garlic, and cook until soft.

2. Add the chicken pieces and brown on all sides.

3. Stir in the tomato paste, chicken broth, ras el hanout, salt, and pepper. Bring to a simmer.

4. Add the potatoes, carrots, chickpeas, and apricots. Cover and cook on low heat for 45 minutes or until the chicken is tender.

5. Garnish with cilantro before serving. Serve hot with bread or couscous.

CHICKEN WITH OLIVES AND CAPERS

Ingredients

- Chicken breasts - 4, boneless and skinless.
- Green olives - 1/2 cup, pitted.
- Capers - 2 tablespoons.
- Garlic cloves - 2, minced.
- White wine - 1/2 cup.
- Chicken broth - 1 cup.
- Lemon - 1, juiced.
- Olive oil - 2 tablespoons.
- Salt and pepper - to taste.
- Parsley - 2 tablespoons, chopped for garnish.

Instructions

1. Season the chicken breasts with salt and pepper.

2. Heat the olive oil in a skillet over medium-high heat. Add the chicken and cook until golden brown on both sides. Remove the chicken from the skillet.

3. In the same skillet, add the garlic, olives, and capers. Cook for 1-2 minutes.

4. Add the white wine and lemon juice, scraping up any browned bits from the bottom of the skillet.

5. Return the chicken to the skillet, add the chicken broth, and bring to a simmer. Cover and cook until the chicken is cooked through.

6. Garnish with parsley before serving.

STUFFED CHICKEN WITH FREEKEH

Ingredients

- Whole chicken - 1, about 1.5 kg.
- Freekeh - 1 cup, cooked according to package instructions.
- Onion - 1, chopped.
- Pine nuts - 1/4 cup.
- Raisins - 1/4 cup.
- Cinnamon - 1 teaspoon.
- Allspice - 1/2 teaspoon.
- Chicken broth - 2 cups.
- Olive oil - 2 tablespoons.
- Salt and pepper - to taste.
- Parsley - 2 tablespoons, chopped for garnish.

Instructions

1. Preheat your oven to 190°C (375°F).

2. In a skillet, heat 1 tablespoon of olive oil over medium heat. Sauté the onion until translucent. Add the pine nuts and raisins, and cook until the pine nuts are golden. Stir in the cooked freekeh, cinnamon, allspice, salt, and pepper.

3. Stuff the chicken with the freekeh mixture. Truss the chicken if desired.

4. Place the stuffed chicken in a roasting pan. Rub the outside with the remaining olive oil and season with salt and pepper.

5. Roast in the preheated oven for 1.5 hours, or until the chicken is cooked through and the skin is golden, basting occasionally with chicken broth.

6. Garnish with parsley before serving. Serve with additional freekeh on the side if desired.

GRILLED CHICKEN WITH HARISSA

Ingredients

- Chicken breasts - 4, boneless and skinless.
- Harissa paste - 3 tablespoons.
- Olive oil - 2 tablespoons.
- Lemon juice - 2 tablespoons.
- Garlic cloves - 2, minced.
- Salt and pepper - to taste.

Instructions

1. In a bowl, mix together the harissa paste, olive oil, lemon juice, minced garlic, salt, and pepper to create a marinade.

2. Coat the chicken breasts evenly with the marinade. Let them marinate in the refrigerator for at least 1 hour, or overnight for best results.

3. Preheat the grill to medium-high heat.

4. Grill the chicken breasts for 6-7 minutes on each side, or until fully cooked and the internal temperature reaches 165°F (74°C).

5. Serve hot, garnished with lemon slices and additional harissa if desired.

CHICKEN AND ALMOND BRIK

Ingredients

- Phyllo dough - 4 sheets.
- Chicken breast - 1, cooked and shredded.
- Almonds - 1/2 cup, toasted and chopped.
- Onion - 1, finely chopped.
- Parsley - 1/4 cup, chopped.
- Egg - 1, beaten.
- Ground cinnamon - 1/2 teaspoon.
- Salt and pepper - to taste.
- Vegetable oil - for frying.

Instructions

1. In a pan, sauté the onion until translucent. Add the shredded chicken, toasted almonds, parsley, ground cinnamon, salt, and pepper. Mix well and cook for a few minutes. Let the mixture cool.

2. Place a spoonful of the chicken mixture onto the center of each phyllo sheet. Add a bit of the beaten egg on top of the filling.

3. Fold the phyllo dough to enclose the filling, forming a triangle shape.

4. Heat oil in a frying pan over medium heat. Fry each brik until golden brown on both sides.

5. Drain on paper towels and serve hot.

TUNISIAN CHICKEN KEBABS

Ingredients

- Chicken breasts - 2, cut into cubes.
- Yogurt - 1/2 cup.
- Harissa paste - 2 tablespoons.
- Garlic cloves - 2, minced.
- Cumin - 1 teaspoon.
- Coriander - 1 teaspoon.
- Olive oil - 1 tablespoon.
- Salt and pepper - to taste.
- Wooden skewers - soaked in water for 30 minutes.

Instructions

1. In a bowl, combine the yogurt, harissa paste, minced garlic, cumin, coriander, olive oil, salt, and pepper to make a marinade.

2. Add the chicken cubes to the marinade and ensure they are well coated. Cover and refrigerate for at least 2 hours, or overnight.

3. Thread the marinated chicken cubes onto the soaked skewers.

4. Preheat the grill to medium-high heat.

5. Grill the chicken kebabs, turning occasionally, for 10-12 minutes or until fully cooked and charred on the edges.

6. Serve hot, accompanied by fresh salads or grilled vegetables.

CHICKEN LIVER WITH HARISSA ON TOAST

Ingredients

- Chicken livers - 500 grams, cleaned and trimmed.
- Harissa paste - 1 tablespoon.
- Olive oil - 2 tablespoons.
- Garlic cloves - 2, minced.
- Lemon juice - 1 tablespoon.
- Salt and pepper - to taste.
- Bread slices - 4, toasted.
- Fresh parsley - for garnish.

Instructions

1. Heat the olive oil in a skillet over medium heat. Add the minced garlic and sauté until fragrant.

2. Add the chicken livers and cook until they are browned on all sides but still pink in the middle.

3. Stir in the harissa paste, lemon juice, salt, and pepper. Cook for an additional 2-3 minutes.

4. Serve the chicken livers on top of the toasted bread slices.

5. Garnish with fresh parsley and serve immediately.

CHICKEN AND EGGPLANT STEW

Ingredients

- Chicken thighs - 4, bone-in and skin-on.
- Eggplants - 2, cubed.
- Tomatoes - 3, diced.
- Onion - 1, chopped.

- Garlic cloves - 3, minced.
- Chicken broth - 2 cups.
- Tomato paste - 1 tablespoon.
- Paprika - 1 teaspoon.
- Cumin - 1/2 teaspoon.
- Olive oil - 2 tablespoons.
- Salt and pepper - to taste.
- Fresh cilantro - for garnish.

Instructions

1. Heat the olive oil in a large pot over medium heat. Add the chicken thighs, season with salt and pepper, and brown on both sides. Remove and set aside.

2. In the same pot, add the onion and garlic. Cook until the onion is translucent.

3. Add the eggplants and cook for a few minutes until they start to soften.

4. Stir in the tomatoes, tomato paste, paprika, and cumin. Cook for a couple of minutes.

5. Return the chicken to the pot. Add the chicken broth and bring to a boil. Reduce the heat and simmer, covered, for 25-30 minutes or until the chicken is cooked through and the vegetables are tender.

6. Adjust the seasoning as needed. Garnish with fresh cilantro before serving.

CHICKEN MLOUKHIYA

Ingredients

- Chicken pieces - 1 kg.

- Dried mloukhiya (jute leaves) - 100 grams, ground.
- Onion - 1, finely chopped.
- Garlic cloves - 4, minced.
- Ground coriander - 1 teaspoon.
- Ground caraway - 1 teaspoon.
- Chili powder - 1/2 teaspoon.
- Chicken broth - 6 cups.
- Olive oil - 3 tablespoons.
- Salt and pepper - to taste.

Instructions

1. In a large pot, heat the olive oil over medium heat. Add the onions and garlic, and cook until soft.

2. Add the chicken pieces and brown on all sides.

3. Sprinkle the ground mloukhiya, coriander, caraway, and chili powder over the chicken. Stir well to coat the chicken evenly.

4. Pour in the chicken broth, and bring to a boil. Reduce the heat, cover, and simmer for 1 hour, or until the chicken is tender.

5. Season with salt and pepper to taste. Serve hot over rice or with Tunisian bread.

TUNISIAN CHICKEN WITH APRICOTS

Ingredients

- Chicken thighs - 4, bone-in and skin-on.
- Dried apricots - 1 cup.
- Onion - 1, sliced.
- Garlic cloves - 2, minced.
- Chicken stock - 2 cups.

- Honey - 2 tablespoons.
- Cinnamon stick - 1.
- Ground ginger - 1 teaspoon.
- Turmeric - 1/2 teaspoon.
- Olive oil - 2 tablespoons.
- Salt and pepper - to taste.
- Almonds - 1/4 cup, toasted for garnish.

Instructions

1. Preheat the oven to 180°C (356°F).

2. In a large ovenproof skillet, heat the olive oil over medium heat. Season the chicken with salt and pepper, and brown on both sides. Remove from skillet.

3. In the same skillet, add the onion and garlic, and cook until softened.

4. Add the dried apricots, chicken stock, honey, cinnamon stick, ground ginger, and turmeric. Bring to a simmer.

5. Return the chicken to the skillet, and spoon the sauce over the chicken.

6. Cover and bake in the oven for 25-30 minutes, or until the chicken is cooked through.

7. Garnish with toasted almonds before serving.

CHICKEN SHAWARMA TUNISIAN STYLE

Ingredients

- Chicken breasts - 2, thinly sliced.

- Yogurt - 1/2 cup.
- Lemon juice - 2 tablespoons.
- Garlic cloves - 2, minced.
- Ground cumin - 1 teaspoon.
- Paprika - 1 teaspoon.
- Turmeric - 1/2 teaspoon.
- Cayenne pepper - 1/4 teaspoon.
- Salt and pepper - to taste.
- Olive oil - for cooking.
- Flatbreads - for serving.

Instructions

1. In a bowl, combine the yogurt, lemon juice, garlic, cumin, paprika, turmeric, cayenne, salt, and pepper. Add the chicken and toss to coat. Marinate for at least 1 hour, or overnight for best results.

2. Heat a grill pan or skillet over medium-high heat with a bit of olive oil. Add the chicken slices and cook for 5-7 minutes on each side, or until fully cooked.

3. Serve the chicken shawarma wrapped in flatbreads, accompanied by your choice of toppings such as tomatoes, cucumbers, onions, and tahini sauce.

ROASTED DUCK WITH DATES

Ingredients

- Duck - 1 whole, about 2 kg.
- Dates - 1 cup, pitted.
- Oranges - 2, one juiced and one sliced.
- Onion - 1, quartered.
- Garlic cloves - 4, whole.
- Cinnamon stick - 1.
- Star anise - 2.

- Salt and pepper - to taste.
- Olive oil - 2 tablespoons.

Instructions

1. Preheat the oven to 200°C (390°F).

2. Season the inside and outside of the duck with salt and pepper. Stuff the cavity with the dates, orange slices, onion quarters, whole garlic cloves, cinnamon stick, and star anise.

3. Place the duck breast-side up in a roasting pan. Drizzle with olive oil and orange juice.

4. Roast in the preheated oven for 1 hour and 30 minutes, or until the skin is crispy and the meat is cooked through, basting occasionally with the pan juices.

5. Let the duck rest for 10 minutes before carving. Serve with the roasted dates and additional orange slices.

CHICKEN AND FIG TAGINE

Ingredients

- Chicken thighs - 6, bone-in and skin-on.
- Dried figs - 1 cup.
- Onion - 1, finely chopped.
- Garlic cloves - 2, minced.
- Chicken broth - 2 cups.
- Honey - 2 tablespoons.
- Cinnamon - 1 teaspoon.
- Ginger - 1/2 teaspoon, ground.
- Saffron - a pinch.
- Salt and pepper - to taste.
- Almonds - 1/2 cup, toasted and sliced for garnish.

- Olive oil - 2 tablespoons.

Instructions

1. In a tagine or large pot, heat the olive oil over medium heat. Add the onions and garlic, and cook until soft.

2. Season the chicken with salt and pepper, add to the pot, and brown on all sides.

3. Add the dried figs, chicken broth, honey, cinnamon, ginger, and saffron. Bring to a simmer.

4. Cover and cook on low heat for 45 minutes to 1 hour, or until the chicken is tender.

5. Garnish with toasted sliced almonds before serving.

CHICKEN PASTILLA

Ingredients

- Chicken thighs - 4, boneless and skinless.
- Phyllo pastry - 8 sheets.
- Almonds - 1 cup, blanched and chopped.
- Onion - 1, finely chopped.
- Cinnamon - 1 teaspoon.
- Ginger powder - 1/2 teaspoon.
- Saffron threads - a pinch.
- Eggs - 2, beaten.
- Powdered sugar - 1/4 cup, plus extra for dusting.
- Butter - 1/2 cup, melted.
- Salt and pepper - to taste.

Instructions

1. Cook the chicken thighs in a pan with salt, pepper,

ginger, saffron, and enough water to cover. Once cooked, shred the meat and set aside.

2. In the same pan, sauté the onion until translucent. Add the shredded chicken, almonds, cinnamon, and powdered sugar. Cook for a few minutes, then let cool. Mix in the beaten eggs.

3. Preheat the oven to 180°C (356°F). Brush a pie dish with melted butter and layer 4 phyllo sheets, brushing each with butter and overlapping them in the dish.

4. Add the chicken mixture to the dish, then cover with the remaining phyllo sheets, brushing each with butter. Tuck the edges to seal the filling inside.

5. Bake for 25-30 minutes, or until golden brown. Dust with powdered sugar before serving.

CHICKEN WITH CHICKPEAS AND HARISSA

Ingredients

- Chicken breasts - 2, cubed.
- Chickpeas - 1 can, drained and rinsed.
- Harissa paste - 2 tablespoons.
- Garlic cloves - 2, minced.
- Tomatoes - 2, diced.
- Chicken stock - 1 cup.
- Coriander - 1 teaspoon, ground.
- Cumin - 1 teaspoon, ground.
- Olive oil - 2 tablespoons.
- Salt and pepper - to taste.
- Cilantro - for garnish.

Instructions

1. Heat the olive oil in a skillet over medium heat. Add the chicken cubes and cook until browned. Remove and set aside.

2. In the same skillet, add garlic and cook until fragrant. Stir in the harissa, tomatoes, coriander, and cumin. Cook for a few minutes.

3. Add the chickpeas and chicken stock. Bring to a simmer.

4. Return the chicken to the skillet. Cover and simmer until the chicken is cooked through and the sauce has thickened, about 15 minutes.

5. Season with salt and pepper. Garnish with cilantro before serving.

TUNISIAN JERK CHICKEN

Ingredients

- Chicken legs - 4.
- Jerk seasoning - 2 tablespoons.
- Garlic powder - 1 teaspoon.
- Olive oil - 3 tablespoons.
- Lime juice - 2 tablespoons.
- Honey - 1 tablespoon.
- Salt and pepper - to taste.

Instructions

1. In a bowl, mix together the jerk seasoning, garlic powder, olive oil, lime juice, honey, salt, and pepper.

2. Rub the mixture all over the chicken legs. Let them marinate in the refrigerator for at least 2 hours, or overnight for best results.

3. Preheat the oven to 200°C (392°F). Place the chicken legs on a baking sheet.

4. Bake for 35-40 minutes, or until the chicken is cooked through and the skin is crispy.

5. Serve hot.

CHICKEN AND POTATO GRATIN

Ingredients

- Chicken breasts - 2, sliced thinly.
- Potatoes - 3, sliced thinly.
- Heavy cream - 1 cup.
- Garlic cloves - 2, minced.
- Nutmeg - 1/4 teaspoon, grated.
- Grated cheese - 1 cup.
- Salt and pepper - to taste.
- Butter - for greasing.

Instructions

1. Preheat the oven to 180°C (356°F). Grease a baking dish with butter.

2. Layer the potatoes and chicken slices alternately in the dish, seasoning each layer with salt, pepper, and minced garlic.

3. Pour the heavy cream over the layers and sprinkle with grated nutmeg.

4. Top with grated cheese and cover with foil.

5. Bake for 1 hour, then remove the foil and bake for another 15-20 minutes, or until the top is golden and bubbly. Serve hot.

CHICKEN WITH PRESERVED LEMON AND OLIVES

Ingredients

- Chicken thighs - 4, bone-in and skin-on.
- Preserved lemons - 2, sliced.
- Green olives - 1/2 cup.
- Onion - 1, sliced.
- Garlic cloves - 2, minced.
- Chicken broth - 1 cup.
- Saffron threads - a pinch.
- Paprika - 1 teaspoon.
- Olive oil - 2 tablespoons.
- Salt and pepper - to taste.
- Cilantro - for garnish.

Instructions

1. Heat the olive oil in a skillet over medium heat. Add the chicken thighs, season with salt and pepper, and brown on both sides. Remove and set aside.

2. In the same skillet, add the onion and garlic. Cook until the onion is soft.

3. Return the chicken to the skillet. Add the preserved lemons, olives, chicken broth, saffron, and paprika.

4. Cover and simmer for 30 minutes, or until the chicken is cooked through. Garnish with cilantro before serving.

LAMB DISHES

Lamb in Tunisian cuisine occupies a distinguished position, offering unique flavors that set it apart from other culinary elements. It is celebrated for its nutritional richness, providing a significant source of protein, vitamins, and minerals essential for a balanced diet. The flexibility of lamb within Tunisian dishes is unparalleled, showcased in an array of preparations from slow-cooked stews to grilled skewers, each method enhancing the meat's natural flavors with the country's signature spices.

The incorporation of lamb into Tunisian cooking goes beyond mere sustenance; it represents a fusion of tradition and taste that is central to the country's gastronomic identity. Lamb dishes serve as a culinary exploration of Tunisia's rich heritage, blending aromatic herbs and spices to create meals that are both comforting and sophisticated. This culinary tradition underscores the importance of lamb in promoting a diet that is not only rich in flavor but also in health benefits, making it a preferred choice for those seeking wholesome, flavorful meals.

Lamb is a cornerstone of Tunisian cuisine, vital for anyone aiming to combine the joys of eating well with the principles of nutritious living. Its role within the culinary landscape underscores an ongoing commitment to dishes that satisfy the palate while supporting overall health.

LAMB COUSCOUS

Ingredients

- Lamb shoulder - 1 kg, cubed.
- Couscous - 2 cups.

- Carrots - 2, sliced.
- Zucchini - 2, sliced.
- Chickpeas - 1 cup, soaked overnight and drained.
- Onion - 1, chopped.
- Tomato paste - 2 tablespoons.
- Harissa - 1 tablespoon.
- Chicken broth - 4 cups.
- Ras el hanout - 1 teaspoon.
- Salt and pepper - to taste.
- Olive oil - 2 tablespoons.

Instructions

1. In a large pot, brown the lamb cubes in olive oil. Add the onions and sauté until translucent.

2. Stir in the tomato paste, harissa, ras el hanout, salt, and pepper. Add enough chicken broth to cover the meat, bring to a boil, then reduce heat and simmer for 1 hour.

3. Add the carrots, zucchini, and chickpeas to the pot. Continue to simmer until the vegetables are tender.

4. Prepare the couscous according to package instructions, using the remaining chicken broth as the liquid.

5. Serve the lamb and vegetables over the couscous, with some of the broth spooned over the top.

GRILLED LAMB CHOPS WITH HARISSA

Ingredients

- Lamb chops - 8.
- Harissa paste - 3 tablespoons.
- Olive oil - 4 tablespoons.

- Garlic cloves - 2, minced.
- Lemon juice - 2 tablespoons.
- Salt and pepper - to taste.

Instructions

1. In a bowl, mix together the harissa paste, olive oil, minced garlic, lemon juice, salt, and pepper. Coat the lamb chops with this mixture and let them marinate for at least 2 hours, or overnight in the refrigerator.

2. Preheat the grill to medium-high heat. Grill the lamb chops for 3-4 minutes on each side for medium-rare, or longer to your desired level of doneness.

3. Let the lamb chops rest for a few minutes before serving.

LAMB SHANK TAGINE

Ingredients

- Lamb shanks - 4.
- Onions - 2, chopped.
- Garlic cloves - 4, minced.
- Carrots - 2, sliced.
- Dried apricots - 1/2 cup.
- Chicken broth - 3 cups.
- Turmeric - 1 teaspoon.
- Cinnamon stick - 1.
- Ginger - 1 tablespoon, grated.
- Saffron threads - a pinch.
- Salt and pepper - to taste.
- Olive oil - 2 tablespoons.

Instructions

1. In a tagine or large pot, heat the olive oil over medium heat. Brown the lamb shanks on all sides, then remove and set aside.

2. In the same pot, add the onions and garlic, cooking until softened. Add the carrots, dried apricots, turmeric, cinnamon stick, ginger, and saffron.

3. Return the lamb shanks to the pot. Add the chicken broth and season with salt and pepper.

4. Cover and simmer for 2-3 hours, or until the lamb is very tender.

5. Serve the lamb shanks with the sauce and vegetables, garnished with fresh cilantro or parsley if desired.

SPICED LAMB KEBABS

Ingredients

- Lamb - 500 grams, cubed.
- Cumin - 2 teaspoons.
- Paprika - 1 teaspoon.
- Coriander - 1 teaspoon, ground.
- Garlic powder - 1/2 teaspoon.
- Olive oil - 3 tablespoons.
- Lemon juice - 2 tablespoons.
- Salt and pepper - to taste.

Instructions

1. In a bowl, combine the cumin, paprika, coriander, garlic powder, olive oil, lemon juice, salt, and pepper. Add the lamb cubes and toss to coat evenly. Marinate for at

least 1 hour, or overnight in the refrigerator.

2. Thread the marinated lamb cubes onto skewers.

3. Preheat the grill to medium-high heat. Grill the kebabs, turning occasionally, until cooked to your liking, about 10-15 minutes for medium-rare.

4. Serve the kebabs hot, garnished with fresh herbs and lemon wedges.

LAMB MLOUKHIYA

Ingredients

- Lamb - 1 kg, cut into pieces.
- Dried mloukhiya leaves - 100 grams, ground.
- Garlic cloves - 6, minced.
- Coriander seeds - 1 tablespoon, ground.
- Chicken broth - 6 cups.
- Olive oil - 4 tablespoons.
- Salt and pepper - to taste.

Instructions

1. In a large pot, heat the olive oil over medium heat. Add the lamb pieces and brown on all sides.

2. Add the minced garlic and ground coriander, and cook for another minute.

3. Cover the lamb with chicken broth and bring to a boil. Reduce heat to low, cover, and simmer for 1 hour.

4. Stir in the ground mloukhiya leaves and continue to simmer for another hour, or until the lamb is tender and the sauce has thickened.

5. Season with salt and pepper to taste. Serve hot, accompanied by Tunisian bread or rice.

LAMB AND PRUNE STEW

Ingredients

- Lamb - 1 kg, cubed.
- Prunes - 200 grams.
- Onions - 2, finely chopped.
- Garlic cloves - 3, minced.
- Ground cinnamon - 1 teaspoon.
- Ground ginger - 1 teaspoon.
- Saffron threads - a pinch.
- Chicken broth - 4 cups.
- Almonds - 100 grams, toasted.
- Honey - 2 tablespoons.
- Sesame seeds - 1 tablespoon, for garnish.
- Salt and pepper - to taste.
- Olive oil - 3 tablespoons.

Instructions

1. In a large pot, heat the olive oil over medium heat. Add the onions and garlic, and sauté until they begin to soften.

2. Add the lamb cubes and brown on all sides. Stir in the cinnamon, ginger, and saffron, cooking for a few minutes until fragrant.

3. Pour in the chicken broth, bring to a boil, then reduce the heat and simmer for 1.5 hours, or until the lamb is tender.

4. Add the prunes and honey, and continue to simmer for another 30 minutes. Adjust seasoning with salt and pepper.

5. Serve hot, garnished with toasted almonds and sesame seeds.

ROASTED LAMB SHOULDER WITH ROSEMARY

Ingredients

- Lamb shoulder - 2 kg.
- Fresh rosemary - 3 sprigs.
- Garlic cloves - 4, sliced.
- Olive oil - 4 tablespoons.
- White wine - 1 cup.
- Salt and pepper - to taste.

Instructions

1. Preheat the oven to 190°C (375°F).

2. Make small incisions in the lamb shoulder and insert slices of garlic and rosemary sprigs.

3. Rub the entire lamb shoulder with olive oil, salt, and pepper, ensuring it's evenly coated.

4. Place the lamb in a roasting pan and pour the white wine around it.

5. Roast in the preheated oven for about 2.5 to 3 hours, or until the lamb is tender and well-cooked. Baste with the pan juices every 30 minutes to keep it moist.

6. Once done, let the lamb rest for 15 minutes before slicing. Serve with the pan juices drizzled over the top.

LAMB AND CHICKPEA STEW

Ingredients

- Lamb - 800 grams, cubed.
- Chickpeas - 1 can (400 grams), drained and rinsed.
- Onions - 2, chopped.
- Garlic cloves - 3, minced.
- Tomato paste - 2 tablespoons.
- Ground cumin - 1 teaspoon.
- Ground coriander - 1 teaspoon.
- Chicken or vegetable broth - 4 cups.
- Fresh cilantro - 1/4 cup, chopped.
- Salt and pepper - to taste.
- Olive oil - 2 tablespoons.

Instructions

1. Heat the olive oil in a large pot over medium heat. Add the onions and garlic, and sauté until soft and translucent.

2. Increase the heat to medium-high, add the lamb cubes, and brown on all sides.

3. Stir in the tomato paste, cumin, and coriander, cooking for a few minutes to develop the flavors.

4. Add the chickpeas and broth. Bring to a boil, then reduce the heat, cover, and simmer for 1 hour or until the lamb is tender.

5. Season with salt and pepper. Stir in the fresh cilantro just before serving.

LAMB TAGINE WITH APRICOTS

Ingredients

- Lamb shanks - 4.
- Dried apricots - 150 grams.
- Onions - 2, sliced.
- Garlic cloves - 4, minced.
- Ground cinnamon - 1 teaspoon.
- Ground ginger - 1 teaspoon.
- Saffron threads - a pinch.
- Chicken stock - 3 cups.
- Honey - 2 tablespoons.
- Almonds - 50 grams, blanched and toasted.
- Salt and pepper - to taste.
- Olive oil - 3 tablespoons.

Instructions

1. In a tagine or large pot, heat the olive oil over medium heat. Add the onions and garlic, and cook until they start to soften.

2. Add the lamb shanks and brown on all sides. Sprinkle with cinnamon, ginger, and saffron, and cook for a few more minutes.

3. Cover with chicken stock, bring to a boil, then reduce to a simmer. Cover and cook for 1.5 hours.

4. Add the dried apricots and honey. Continue to simmer for 30 minutes or until the lamb is very tender and the sauce has thickened.

5. Season with salt and pepper. Garnish with toasted almonds before serving.

LAMB SAUSAGE WITH HARISSA

Ingredients

- Lamb sausage - 500 grams.
- Harissa paste - 2 tablespoons.
- Olive oil - 2 tablespoons.
- Onions - 2, sliced.
- Garlic cloves - 2, minced.
- Red bell peppers - 2, sliced.
- Salt and pepper - to taste.

Instructions

1. In a large skillet, heat the olive oil over medium heat. Add the lamb sausage and cook until browned on all sides.

2. Remove the sausage and set aside. In the same skillet, add the onions, garlic, and red bell peppers. Sauté until the vegetables are soft.

3. Stir in the harissa paste and cook for a few more minutes, allowing the flavors to meld.

4. Return the sausage to the skillet. Season with salt and pepper, and cook for an additional 5-10 minutes, or until the sausage is cooked through.

5. Serve hot, with a side of couscous or bread.

LAMB MEATBALLS IN TOMATO SAUCE

Ingredients

- Lamb - 500 grams, ground.
- Breadcrumbs - 1/2 cup.

- Egg - 1.
- Garlic cloves - 2, minced.
- Cumin - 1 teaspoon.
- Paprika - 1 teaspoon.
- Salt and pepper - to taste.
- Tomato sauce - 2 cups.
- Olive oil - 2 tablespoons.
- Onion - 1, finely chopped.
- Cilantro - 1/4 cup, chopped for garnish.

Instructions

1. In a bowl, combine ground lamb, breadcrumbs, egg, half of the minced garlic, cumin, paprika, salt, and pepper. Mix well and form into small meatballs.

2. Heat olive oil in a large skillet over medium heat. Brown the meatballs on all sides, then remove and set aside.

3. In the same skillet, add the onion and the remaining garlic, cooking until soft. Add the tomato sauce and bring to a simmer.

4. Return the meatballs to the skillet, cover, and simmer for 20 minutes, or until the meatballs are cooked through.

5. Garnish with chopped cilantro before serving.

STUFFED LAMB WITH RICE AND NUTS

Ingredients

- Lamb shoulder - 1 kg, deboned.
- Rice - 1 cup, cooked.
- Pine nuts - 1/4 cup, toasted.

- Almonds - 1/4 cup, toasted and chopped.
- Raisins - 1/4 cup.
- Onion - 1, finely chopped.
- Allspice - 1 teaspoon.
- Cinnamon - 1/2 teaspoon.
- Salt and pepper - to taste.
- Chicken broth - 2 cups.
- Olive oil - 2 tablespoons.

Instructions

1. Preheat the oven to 180°C (356°F).

2. In a bowl, mix the cooked rice, pine nuts, almonds, raisins, onion, allspice, cinnamon, salt, and pepper.

3. Stuff the lamb shoulder with the rice mixture and tie it up with kitchen twine to secure.

4. In a roasting pan, heat the olive oil over medium heat. Brown the lamb on all sides.

5. Add the chicken broth to the pan and bring to a simmer. Cover with foil and transfer to the oven.

6. Roast for about 2 hours, or until the lamb is tender. Baste occasionally with the pan juices.

7. Let rest before slicing. Serve with the pan juices.

LAMB AND SPINACH STEW

Ingredients

- Lamb - 500 grams, cubed.
- Spinach - 500 grams, washed and chopped.
- Onion - 1, chopped.

- Garlic cloves - 2, minced.
- Tomato paste - 2 tablespoons.
- Chicken broth - 3 cups.
- Coriander - 1 teaspoon, ground.
- Cumin - 1 teaspoon.
- Olive oil - 2 tablespoons.
- Salt and pepper - to taste.

Instructions

1. Heat the olive oil in a large pot over medium heat. Add the onion and garlic, and cook until soft.

2. Add the lamb and brown on all sides.

3. Stir in the tomato paste, coriander, and cumin. Cook for a few minutes, stirring constantly.

4. Add the chicken broth and bring to a boil. Reduce heat, cover, and simmer for 1 hour, or until the lamb is tender.

5. Add the spinach and cook until wilted. Season with salt and pepper.

6. Serve hot.

LAMB SHANK WITH SAFFRON

Ingredients

- Lamb shanks - 4.
- Saffron threads - a pinch, soaked in 2 tablespoons warm water.
- Onion - 1, chopped.
- Garlic cloves - 3, minced.
- Chicken broth - 4 cups.
- White wine - 1 cup.

- Olive oil - 2 tablespoons.
- Salt and pepper - to taste.
- Fresh cilantro - for garnish.

Instructions

1. Preheat the oven to 160°C (320°F).

2. Heat the olive oil in a large ovenproof pot over medium heat. Season the lamb shanks with salt and pepper, and brown on all sides. Remove and set aside.

3. In the same pot, add the onion and garlic, cooking until soft.

4. Return the lamb shanks to the pot. Add the saffron with its soaking water, chicken broth, and white wine. Bring to a simmer.

5. Cover and transfer to the oven. Cook for 2 to 2.5 hours, or until the lamb is falling off the bone.

6. Garnish with fresh cilantro before serving.

BRAISED LAMB WITH FENNEL

Ingredients

- Lamb - 1 kg, cubed.
- Fennel bulbs - 2, sliced.
- Onion - 1, sliced.
- Garlic cloves - 3, minced.
- White wine - 1 cup.
- Chicken broth - 2 cups.
- Thyme - 1 teaspoon, dried.
- Olive oil - 3 tablespoons.
- Salt and pepper - to taste.

- Lemon zest - from 1 lemon.

Instructions

1. Heat the olive oil in a large pot over medium-high heat. Season the lamb with salt and pepper, and brown in batches. Remove and set aside.

2. In the same pot, add the fennel and onion, cooking until soft. Add the garlic and cook for another minute.

3. Return the lamb to the pot. Add the white wine and scrape up any browned bits from the bottom of the pot.

4. Add the chicken broth and thyme. Bring to a boil, then reduce heat, cover, and simmer for 1.5 hours, or until the lamb is tender.

5. Stir in the lemon zest before serving. Serve hot.

LAMB BRIK

Ingredients

- Lamb mince - 500 grams.
- Onion - 1, finely chopped.
- Parsley - 1/4 cup, chopped.
- Harissa - 1 teaspoon.
- Egg - 1.
- Brik pastry sheets - 4.
- Salt and pepper - to taste.
- Oil - for frying.

Instructions

1. In a bowl, combine the lamb mince, onion, parsley, harissa, egg, salt, and pepper. Mix well.

2. Place a portion of the lamb mixture onto the center of each brik pastry sheet.

3. Fold the pastry over the filling to create a triangle or envelope shape, sealing the edges well.

4. Heat oil in a frying pan over medium heat. Fry each brik until golden brown on both sides.

5. Serve hot, ideally with lemon wedges and additional harissa on the side.

LAMB WITH ARTICHOKES AND PEAS

Ingredients

- Lamb - 800 grams, cut into chunks.
- Artichoke hearts - 8, quartered.
- Frozen peas - 1 cup.
- Onion - 1, chopped.
- Garlic cloves - 2, minced.
- Chicken stock - 2 cups.
- Lemon juice - 2 tablespoons.
- Olive oil - 2 tablespoons.
- Salt and pepper - to taste.
- Fresh mint - for garnish.

Instructions

1. Heat olive oil in a large pot over medium heat. Add the lamb chunks and brown on all sides. Remove and set aside.

2. In the same pot, sauté the onion and garlic until soft.

3. Return the lamb to the pot, add the chicken stock, and bring to a boil. Lower the heat, cover, and simmer for 1

hour.

4. Add the artichoke hearts and peas, and cook for an additional 20 minutes, or until the vegetables are tender.

5. Stir in the lemon juice, and season with salt and pepper.

6. Garnish with fresh mint before serving.

LAMB LIVER WITH SPICES

Ingredients

- Lamb liver - 500 grams, sliced.
- Cumin - 1 teaspoon.
- Coriander - 1 teaspoon, ground.
- Paprika - 1/2 teaspoon.
- Turmeric - 1/4 teaspoon.
- Garlic powder - 1/2 teaspoon.
- Salt and pepper - to taste.
- Olive oil - 2 tablespoons.

Instructions

1. In a bowl, mix together cumin, coriander, paprika, turmeric, garlic powder, salt, and pepper.

2. Coat the lamb liver slices in the spice mixture.

3. Heat olive oil in a skillet over medium-high heat. Add the liver slices and cook for 2-3 minutes on each side, or until cooked to your preference.

4. Serve hot, garnished with fresh herbs if desired.

GRILLED LAMB WITH MINT

Ingredients

- Lamb chops - 8.
- Fresh mint - 1/2 cup, chopped.
- Garlic cloves - 2, minced.
- Olive oil - 3 tablespoons.
- Lemon juice - 2 tablespoons.
- Salt and pepper - to taste.

Instructions

1. In a bowl, combine the chopped mint, minced garlic, olive oil, lemon juice, salt, and pepper. Mix well.

2. Marinate the lamb chops in the mint mixture for at least 1 hour, or overnight in the refrigerator for best flavor.

3. Preheat the grill to medium-high heat.

4. Grill the lamb chops for 3-4 minutes on each side for medium-rare, or to your desired level of doneness.

5. Serve hot, garnished with additional fresh mint.

LAMB AND EGGPLANT TAGINE

Ingredients

- Lamb - 1 kg, cut into pieces.
- Eggplants - 2, diced.
- Onion - 1, chopped.
- Garlic cloves - 3, minced.
- Tomatoes - 3, diced.
- Chicken stock - 3 cups.

- Cinnamon stick - 1.
- Cumin - 1 teaspoon.
- Paprika - 1 teaspoon.
- Saffron threads - a pinch.
- Olive oil - 2 tablespoons.
- Salt and pepper - to taste.
- Fresh cilantro - for garnish.

Instructions

1. Heat olive oil in a tagine or large pot over medium heat. Add the onion and garlic, and cook until soft.

2. Add the lamb pieces and brown on all sides.

3. Stir in the tomatoes, cinnamon stick, cumin, paprika, and saffron. Cook for a few minutes until fragrant.

4. Add the diced eggplants and chicken stock. Season with salt and pepper.

5. Cover and simmer for 1.5 to 2 hours, or until the lamb is tender and the sauce has thickened.

6. Garnish with fresh cilantro before serving. Serve with couscous or bread.

BEEF DISHES

Beef holds a distinctive place within Tunisian cuisine, characterized by its unique contribution to the country's rich tapestry of flavors. It is prized for its nutritional content, offering a hearty source of protein along with essential vitamins and minerals conducive to a healthy diet. The adaptability of beef in Tunisian recipes is noteworthy, with its use spanning from slow-simmered stews to grilled delicacies, each dish imbued with the vibrant spices and herbs endemic to Tunisian culinary tradition.

In the realm of Tunisian gastronomy, beef is not just an ingredient; it's a medium through which the depth of traditional flavors and cooking techniques are explored and celebrated. The integration of beef into the cuisine reflects a harmonious blend of taste and nutrition, creating dishes that are both satisfying and healthful. This practice exemplifies the Tunisian commitment to meals that delight the senses while fostering well-being, highlighting beef's role in a balanced culinary culture.

Beef's significance in Tunisian cuisine underscores the nation's dedication to offering meals that are as nourishing as they are flavorful. Its presence in the culinary landscape is a testament to the value placed on dishes that provide both gustatory pleasure and nutritional benefits.

BEEF COUSCOUS

Ingredients

- Beef chuck - 1lb.
- Couscous - 2 cups.

- Carrots - 3, chopped.
- Zucchini - 2, sliced.
- Chickpeas - 1 can.
- Tomato paste - 2 tbsp.
- Cumin - 1 tsp.
- Coriander - 1 tsp.
- Chicken broth - 4 cups.
- Onion - 1, diced.
- Garlic - 2 cloves, minced.
- Salt and pepper to taste.

Instructions

1. In a large pot, brown the beef over medium heat and set aside.

2. In the same pot, add onions and garlic, cooking until softened.

3. Stir in tomato paste, cumin, coriander, salt, and pepper, cooking for 2 minutes.

4. Add carrots, zucchini, chickpeas, and browned beef back to the pot.

5. Pour in chicken broth and bring to a boil. Reduce heat and simmer for 1 hour.

6. Cook couscous according to package instructions.

7. Serve the vegetable and beef stew over the couscous.

TUNISIAN BEEF STEW

Ingredients

- Beef stew meat - 2 lbs.

- Onions - 2, chopped.
- Garlic - 4 cloves, minced.
- Potatoes - 3, cubed.
- Carrots - 2, chopped.
- Tomatoes - 2, diced.
- Beef broth - 4 cups.
- Paprika - 1 tbsp.
- Harissa paste - 2 tsp.
- Olive oil - 2 tbsp.
- Salt and pepper to taste.

Instructions

1. Heat olive oil in a pot and brown the beef on all sides.

2. Add onions and garlic, cooking until softened.

3. Stir in paprika, harissa, salt, and pepper.

4. Add potatoes, carrots, and tomatoes to the pot.

5. Pour in beef broth and bring to a boil. Reduce heat and simmer for 2 hours or until beef is tender.

6. Adjust seasoning as needed and serve hot.

BEEF TAGINE WITH POTATOES

Ingredients

- Beef chuck - 1.5 lbs., cut into chunks.
- Potatoes - 4, cubed.
- Onion - 1, finely chopped.
- Garlic - 3 cloves, minced.
- Carrots - 2, chopped.
- Canned tomatoes - 1 can.
- Beef broth - 3 cups.

- Cinnamon - 1 tsp.
- Ginger - 1 tsp.
- Turmeric - 1 tsp.
- Olive oil - 2 tbsp.
- Salt and pepper to taste.

Instructions

1. In a tagine or heavy pot, heat olive oil and brown the beef chunks.

2. Add onion and garlic, cooking until onion is translucent.

3. Stir in cinnamon, ginger, turmeric, salt, and pepper.

4. Add potatoes, carrots, canned tomatoes, and beef broth.

5. Cover and simmer on low heat for 2 hours or until beef is tender.

6. Serve warm, garnished with fresh cilantro if desired.

SPICY BEEF WITH VEGETABLES

Ingredients

- Beef sirloin - 1 lb., thinly sliced.
- Bell peppers - 2, sliced.
- Broccoli - 1 head, cut into florets.
- Carrot - 1, sliced.
- Onion - 1, sliced.
- Garlic - 2 cloves, minced.
- Soy sauce - 1/4 cup.
- Oyster sauce - 2 tbsp.
- Chili flakes - 1 tsp.

- Sesame oil - 2 tbsp.
- Salt and pepper to taste.

Instructions

1. In a wok or large pan, heat sesame oil over high heat.

2. Add beef and stir-fry until browned. Remove and set aside.

3. In the same pan, add garlic, onions, bell peppers, broccoli, and carrot. Stir-fry until vegetables are tender-crisp.

4. Return the beef to the pan. Add soy sauce, oyster sauce, and chili flakes. Stir well to combine.

5. Season with salt and pepper. Serve hot.

BEEF AND BARLEY SOUP

Ingredients

- Beef chuck - 1 lb., cubed.
- Barley - 1 cup.
- Carrots - 2, diced.
- Celery - 2 stalks, diced.
- Onion - 1, diced.
- Garlic - 2 cloves, minced.
- Beef broth - 6 cups.
- Tomato paste - 2 tbsp.
- Thyme - 1 tsp.
- Bay leaves - 2.
- Salt and pepper to taste.

Instructions

1. In a large pot, brown beef over medium heat and set aside.

2. In the same pot, add onions, carrots, celery, and garlic, cooking until softened.

3. Return the beef to the pot along with barley, beef broth, tomato paste, thyme, bay leaves, salt, and pepper.

4. Bring to a boil, then reduce heat and simmer for about 1 hour or until barley and beef are tender.

5. Remove bay leaves before serving. Serve hot.

BEEF KEBABS WITH HARISSA

Ingredients

- Beef - 2 lbs., cut into cubes.
- Harissa paste - 3 tbsp.
- Olive oil - 2 tbsp.
- Garlic - 2 cloves, minced.
- Cumin - 1 tsp.
- Coriander - 1 tsp.
- Salt and pepper to taste.

Instructions

1. In a bowl, mix harissa paste, olive oil, garlic, cumin, coriander, salt, and pepper.

2. Add the beef cubes to the marinade and mix well. Cover and refrigerate for at least 2 hours.

3. Thread the beef cubes onto skewers.

4. Preheat the grill to medium-high heat and grill the

kebabs for 10-15 minutes, turning occasionally, until cooked to desired doneness.

5. Serve hot.

BEEF BRIK

Ingredients

- Ground beef - 1 lb.
- Onion - 1, finely chopped.
- Parsley - 1/4 cup, chopped.
- Eggs - 4.
- Phyllo dough - 8 sheets.
- Salt and pepper to taste.
- Oil for frying.

Instructions

1. In a skillet, cook the ground beef and onions over medium heat until the beef is browned. Drain any excess fat.

2. Stir in parsley, salt, and pepper. Set aside to cool.

3. Place a spoonful of the beef mixture onto the center of a phyllo sheet. Make a well in the center and crack an egg into it. Fold the phyllo to form a triangle, sealing the edges with water.

4. Heat oil in a frying pan and fry each brik until golden brown on both sides.

5. Serve hot.

BEEF AND CARROT STEW

Ingredients

- Beef chuck - 2 lbs., cubed.
- Carrots - 4, sliced.
- Onion - 1, chopped.
- Garlic - 2 cloves, minced.
- Tomato paste - 2 tbsp.
- Beef broth - 4 cups.
- Bay leaves - 2.
- Thyme - 1 tsp.
- Salt and pepper to taste.
- Oil - 2 tbsp.

Instructions

1. In a large pot, heat oil over medium heat and brown the beef cubes. Remove and set aside.

2. In the same pot, add onions and garlic, cooking until softened.

3. Stir in tomato paste, then add carrots, beef, beef broth, bay leaves, thyme, salt, and pepper.

4. Bring to a boil, then reduce heat and simmer, covered, for about 1.5 hours or until beef is tender.

5. Adjust seasoning to taste and serve hot.

MEATBALL TAGINE WITH EGGS

Ingredients

- Ground beef - 1 lb.
- Onion - 1, grated.

- Parsley - 1/4 cup, chopped.
- Paprika - 1 tsp.
- Cumin - 1 tsp.
- Eggs - 4.
- Tomato sauce - 2 cups.
- Salt and pepper to taste.
- Olive oil - 2 tbsp.

Instructions

1. In a bowl, mix ground beef, half of the grated onion, parsley, paprika, cumin, salt, and pepper.

2. Form the mixture into small meatballs.

3. Heat olive oil in a tagine or skillet over medium heat. Cook the meatballs and the rest of the onions until meatballs are browned.

4. Add tomato sauce and simmer for 20 minutes.

5. Crack the eggs over the meatballs. Cover and cook until eggs are set.

6. Serve hot.

BEEF LIVER WITH CUMIN

Ingredients

- Beef liver - 1 lb., sliced.
- Cumin - 2 tsp.
- Paprika - 1 tsp.
- Olive oil - 2 tbsp.
- Garlic - 2 cloves, minced.
- Lemon juice - 2 tbsp.
- Salt and pepper to taste.

Instructions

1. In a bowl, combine cumin, paprika, salt, pepper, olive oil, garlic, and lemon juice. Add the liver slices and marinate for at least 30 minutes.

2. Heat a pan over medium-high heat and cook the liver slices for 2-3 minutes on each side or until cooked to desired doneness.

3. Serve hot, garnished with additional lemon wedges if desired.

STUFFED BEEF ROLLS

Ingredients

- Beef slices - 8, thinly cut.
- Spinach - 2 cups, blanched.
- Feta cheese - 1 cup, crumbled.
- Pine nuts - 1/4 cup, toasted.
- Garlic - 2 cloves, minced.
- Olive oil - for brushing.
- Salt and pepper to taste.

Instructions

1. Lay out the beef slices and season with salt and pepper.

2. Mix spinach, feta cheese, pine nuts, and garlic in a bowl.

3. Place a spoonful of the spinach mixture on each beef slice and roll tightly.

4. Secure with toothpicks if necessary.

5. Brush each roll with olive oil and grill until cooked to desired doneness, turning occasionally.

6. Serve hot.

BEEF AND TURNIP STEW

Ingredients

- Beef chuck - 2 lbs., cubed.
- Turnips - 3, peeled and cubed.
- Carrots - 2, peeled and sliced.
- Onion - 1, chopped.
- Garlic - 2 cloves, minced.
- Beef broth - 4 cups.
- Bay leaves - 2.
- Thyme - 1 tsp.
- Salt and pepper to taste.
- Olive oil - 2 tbsp.

Instructions

1. In a large pot, heat olive oil over medium heat. Add beef and brown on all sides. Remove beef and set aside.

2. In the same pot, add onion and garlic. Cook until softened.

3. Return beef to the pot, add turnips, carrots, beef broth, bay leaves, thyme, salt, and pepper.

4. Bring to a boil, then reduce heat and simmer, covered, for about 1.5 to 2 hours, or until beef is tender.

5. Adjust seasoning as needed and serve hot.

BEEF SAUSAGE IN TOMATO SAUCE

Ingredients

- Beef sausage - 1 lb., sliced.
- Tomato sauce - 2 cups.
- Onion - 1, diced.
- Garlic - 2 cloves, minced.
- Olive oil - 1 tbsp.
- Red wine - 1/2 cup.
- Sugar - 1 tsp.
- Salt and pepper to taste.
- Basil - 1 tbsp, chopped.

Instructions

1. In a skillet, heat olive oil over medium heat. Add onion and garlic and sauté until softened.

2. Add beef sausage and cook until browned.

3. Pour in tomato sauce and red wine. Add sugar, salt, and pepper.

4. Simmer for 20-30 minutes until the sauce thickens.

5. Stir in basil before serving.

6. Serve hot with pasta or bread.

GRILLED BEEF WITH SPICES

Ingredients

- Beef steaks - 4.
- Cumin - 1 tsp.
- Coriander - 1 tsp.

- Paprika - 1 tsp.
- Garlic powder - 1/2 tsp.
- Olive oil - 2 tbsp.
- Salt and pepper to taste.

Instructions

1. In a bowl, mix cumin, coriander, paprika, garlic powder, salt, and pepper.

2. Rub the spice mixture onto both sides of the beef steaks.

3. Drizzle olive oil over the seasoned steaks.

4. Preheat the grill to medium-high heat and grill the steaks to desired doneness, turning once.

5. Let the steaks rest for a few minutes before serving.

BEEF WITH DRIED FRUITS

Ingredients

- Beef chuck - 2 lbs., cubed.
- Dried apricots - 1 cup.
- Dried prunes - 1 cup.
- Onion - 1, chopped.
- Garlic - 2 cloves, minced.
- Beef broth - 3 cups.
- Cinnamon stick - 1.
- Ground ginger - 1 tsp.
- Salt and pepper to taste.
- Olive oil - 2 tbsp.

Instructions

1. In a large pot, heat olive oil over medium heat. Add beef and brown on all sides. Remove beef and set aside.

2. In the same pot, add onion and garlic. Cook until softened.

3. Return beef to the pot. Add dried apricots, prunes, beef broth, cinnamon stick, ground ginger, salt, and pepper.

4. Bring to a boil, then reduce heat and simmer, covered, for about 2 hours, or until beef is tender and sauce has thickened.

5. Adjust seasoning as needed and serve hot, garnished with additional dried fruits if desired.

BEEF MLOUKHIYA

Ingredients

- Beef chuck - 2 lbs., cubed.
- Mloukhiya (dried jute leaves) - 1 cup.
- Garlic - 4 cloves, minced.
- Coriander seeds - 1 tbsp, ground.
- Beef broth - 6 cups.
- Onion - 1, chopped.
- Bay leaves - 2.
- Salt and pepper to taste.
- Olive oil - 2 tbsp.

Instructions

1. In a large pot, heat olive oil over medium heat. Add onions and garlic, sauté until translucent.

2. Add beef and brown on all sides.

3. Add mloukhiya, coriander, bay leaves, salt, and pepper. Stir well to combine.

4. Pour in beef broth and bring to a boil. Reduce heat to low and simmer for 2-3 hours, or until beef is tender and sauce is thickened.

5. Adjust seasoning as needed and serve hot with bread or rice.

BEEF PASTILLA

Ingredients

- Beef tenderloin - 1 lb., cooked and shredded.
- Filo pastry - 10 sheets.
- Almonds - 1/2 cup, toasted and chopped.
- Onion - 1, finely chopped.
- Parsley - 1/4 cup, chopped.
- Cinnamon - 1 tsp.
- Powdered sugar - 2 tbsp.
- Eggs - 2, beaten.
- Butter - 4 tbsp, melted.
- Salt and pepper to taste.

Instructions

1. Preheat oven to 350°F (175°C).

2. In a bowl, combine beef, almonds, onion, parsley, cinnamon, powdered sugar, eggs, salt, and pepper.

3. Brush a sheet of filo pastry with melted butter, place another sheet on top, and brush again. Repeat until you have 5 layers.

4. Place half of the beef mixture in the center of the filo stack. Fold the edges over to enclose the filling, creating a parcel.

5. Repeat with the remaining filo sheets and beef mixture to make a second parcel.

6. Place the parcels on a baking sheet, brush the tops with more melted butter, and bake for 25-30 minutes, or until golden and crispy.

7. Serve hot, dusted with additional powdered sugar and cinnamon if desired.

BRAISED BEEF WITH ONIONS

Ingredients

- Beef brisket - 3 lbs., cut into large pieces.
- Onions - 4, thinly sliced.
- Garlic - 4 cloves, minced.
- Beef broth - 4 cups.
- Red wine - 1 cup.
- Thyme - 1 tsp, dried.
- Bay leaves - 2.
- Olive oil - 2 tbsp.
- Salt and pepper to taste.

Instructions

1. In a large pot or Dutch oven, heat olive oil over medium-high heat. Add beef and sear on all sides until browned. Remove beef and set aside.

2. In the same pot, add onions and garlic, cook until onions are soft and golden.

3. Return beef to the pot. Add beef broth, red wine, thyme, bay leaves, salt, and pepper.

4. Bring to a boil, then reduce heat to low, cover, and simmer for 2-3 hours, or until beef is very tender.

5. Adjust seasoning as needed and serve hot.

BEEF AND PUMPKIN TAGINE

Ingredients

- Beef chuck - 2 lbs., cubed.
- Pumpkin - 2 lbs., peeled and cubed.
- Onion - 1, chopped.
- Garlic - 3 cloves, minced.
- Cinnamon - 1 stick.
- Ginger - 1 tsp, grated.
- Turmeric - 1 tsp.
- Chicken broth - 3 cups.
- Olive oil - 2 tbsp.
- Salt and pepper to taste.
- Coriander - for garnish.

Instructions

1. In a tagine or large pot, heat olive oil over medium heat. Add onions and garlic, sauté until softened.

2. Add beef and brown on all sides.

3. Stir in cinnamon, ginger, turmeric, salt, and pepper.

4. Add pumpkin and chicken broth. Bring to a boil, then reduce heat to low, cover, and simmer for 1.5 to 2 hours, or until beef and pumpkin are tender.

5. Garnish with coriander and serve hot.

BEEF WITH GREEN BEANS AND TOMATOES

Ingredients

- Beef sirloin - 1.5 lbs., sliced into strips.
- Green beans - 1 lb., trimmed.
- Cherry tomatoes - 1 cup, halved.
- Garlic - 3 cloves, minced.
- Olive oil - 2 tbsp.
- Balsamic vinegar - 2 tbsp.
- Salt and pepper to taste.

Instructions

1. In a large skillet, heat olive oil over medium-high heat. Add beef strips and brown on all sides. Remove beef and set aside.

2. In the same skillet, add green beans and cook for about 3-4 minutes, or until tender-crisp.

3. Add garlic and cherry tomatoes, cook for another 2 minutes.

4. Return beef to the skillet. Add balsamic vinegar, salt, and pepper. Cook for an additional 2 minutes, or until everything is heated through.

5. Serve hot.

GRAIN DISHES

Grain dishes in Tunisian cuisine are distinguished by their distinctive role and characteristics, offering a diversity that sets them apart from other dietary staples. These dishes are highly valued for their nutritional benefits, rich in fiber, vitamins, and minerals that are essential for a balanced diet. Their versatility is a hallmark of Tunisian culinary tradition, with grains like couscous, barley, and wheat forming the foundation of an array of recipes, each flavored with the unique blend of spices and ingredients specific to the region.

The importance of grain dishes in Tunisian food culture extends beyond their health benefits, embodying the essence of Tunisian hospitality and communal dining. These grains are adeptly transformed into meals that are both comforting and intricate, reflecting the country's agricultural heritage and culinary innovation. This segment of Tunisian cuisine showcases the skillful balance between satisfying taste and nutritional value, offering dishes that are integral to a wholesome diet.

Grain dishes stand at the core of Tunisian culinary practices, essential for those prioritizing a diet that marries nutrition with culinary delight. Their prominence within the cuisine speaks to a broader commitment to meals that are healthful, yet rich in flavor and cultural significance.

TRADITIONAL TUNISIAN COUSCOUS

Ingredients

- Couscous - 2 cups.
- Chicken broth - 4 cups.

- Chicken pieces - 4.
- Carrots - 2, chopped.
- Zucchini - 2, chopped.
- Onion - 1, chopped.
- Tomato paste - 2 tbsp.
- Harissa - 1 tbsp.
- Chickpeas - 1 cup, cooked.
- Raisins - 1/2 cup.
- Ground cumin - 1 tsp.
- Salt and pepper to taste.

Instructions

1. In a large pot, bring chicken broth to a boil. Add chicken pieces, carrots, zucchini, onion, tomato paste, harissa, chickpeas, raisins, cumin, salt, and pepper. Simmer until vegetables are tender and chicken is cooked through.

2. Prepare couscous according to package instructions.

3. Serve the vegetable and chicken mixture over couscous.

FREEKEH WITH LAMB

Ingredients

- Freekeh - 2 cups, rinsed.
- Lamb shoulder - 1 lb., cubed.
- Onion - 1, chopped.
- Chicken broth - 4 cups.
- Carrots - 2, diced.
- Bay leaves - 2.
- Cinnamon stick - 1.
- Ground allspice - 1 tsp.
- Salt and pepper to taste.

- Olive oil - 2 tbsp.

Instructions

1. In a large pot, heat olive oil over medium heat. Add lamb and onion, cook until lamb is browned.

2. Add freekeh, chicken broth, carrots, bay leaves, cinnamon stick, allspice, salt, and pepper. Bring to a boil, then reduce heat, cover, and simmer for 1 hour or until freekeh is tender and lamb is cooked through.

3. Remove bay leaves and cinnamon stick before serving.

BARLEY PILAF

Ingredients

- Pearl barley - 1 cup, rinsed.
- Chicken broth - 2 cups.
- Onion - 1, diced.
- Carrots - 2, diced.
- Mushrooms - 1 cup, sliced.
- Garlic - 2 cloves, minced.
- Olive oil - 2 tbsp.
- Salt and pepper to taste.
- Fresh parsley - 1/4 cup, chopped for garnish.

Instructions

1. In a large skillet, heat olive oil over medium heat. Add onion, carrots, mushrooms, and garlic. Sauté until vegetables are tender.

2. Add barley and chicken broth. Bring to a boil, then reduce heat, cover, and simmer for 45 minutes or until barley is tender and liquid is absorbed.

3. Season with salt and pepper. Garnish with parsley before serving.

TUNISIAN RICE PILAF

Ingredients

- Long grain rice - 2 cups, rinsed.
- Chicken broth - 4 cups.
- Onion - 1, finely chopped.
- Garlic - 2 cloves, minced.
- Tomato paste - 1 tbsp.
- Turmeric - 1 tsp.
- Cumin - 1/2 tsp.
- Olive oil - 2 tbsp.
- Salt and pepper to taste.
- Fresh cilantro - 1/4 cup, chopped for garnish.

Instructions

1. In a large pot, heat olive oil over medium heat. Add onion and garlic, cook until softened.

2. Stir in tomato paste, turmeric, and cumin, cook for 1 minute.

3. Add rice, chicken broth, salt, and pepper. Bring to a boil, then reduce heat, cover, and simmer for 20 minutes or until rice is tender and liquid is absorbed.

4. Fluff rice with a fork. Garnish with cilantro before serving.

BULGUR WITH VEGETABLES

Ingredients

- Bulgur - 2 cups.
- Vegetable broth - 4 cups.
- Zucchini - 1, diced.
- Red bell pepper - 1, diced.
- Carrot - 1, diced.
- Onion - 1, diced.
- Garlic - 2 cloves, minced.
- Tomato paste - 2 tbsp.
- Cumin - 1 tsp.
- Olive oil - 2 tbsp.
- Salt and pepper to taste.

Instructions

1. In a large skillet, heat olive oil over medium heat. Add onion and garlic, cook until softened.

2. Add zucchini, red bell pepper, carrot, and cook until just tender.

3. Stir in tomato paste, cumin, salt, and pepper, cook for 1 minute.

4. Add bulgur and vegetable broth. Bring to a boil, then reduce heat, cover, and simmer for 15-20 minutes or until bulgur is tender and liquid is absorbed.

5. Adjust seasoning as needed and serve hot.

COUSCOUS WITH SEAFOOD

Ingredients

- Couscous - 2 cups.
- Fish stock - 4 cups.
- Mixed seafood (shrimp, mussels, squid) - 2 lbs.
- Onion - 1, finely chopped.
- Garlic cloves - 2, minced.
- Tomato paste - 1 tbsp.
- Harissa paste - 1 tsp.
- Cumin - 1 tsp.
- Paprika - 1 tsp.
- Olive oil - 2 tbsp.
- Salt and pepper to taste.
- Fresh parsley - for garnish.

Instructions

1. In a large pot, heat olive oil over medium heat. Add onion and garlic, sauté until softened.

2. Stir in tomato paste, harissa, cumin, paprika, salt, and pepper. Cook for 1 minute.

3. Add fish stock and bring to a boil. Add couscous and reduce heat to low. Cover and simmer for 10 minutes.

4. Add mixed seafood, cover, and cook for an additional 5-10 minutes, or until seafood is cooked through.

5. Fluff couscous with a fork, adjust seasoning if necessary, and garnish with fresh parsley before serving.

QUINOA WITH ROASTED VEGETABLES

Ingredients

- Quinoa - 1 cup.
- Vegetable broth - 2 cups.
- Zucchini - 1, cubed.
- Red bell pepper - 1, cubed.
- Carrot - 1, cubed.
- Red onion - 1, chopped.
- Olive oil - 2 tbsp.
- Salt and pepper to taste.
- Ground cumin - 1 tsp.

Instructions

1. Preheat oven to 400°F (200°C). Toss zucchini, bell pepper, carrot, and onion with olive oil, salt, and pepper.

2. Spread the vegetables on a baking sheet and roast for 20-25 minutes, until tender and slightly caramelized.

3. Meanwhile, rinse quinoa under cold water. In a pot, bring vegetable broth to a boil. Add quinoa and reduce heat to low. Cover and simmer for 15 minutes, or until liquid is absorbed.

4. Fluff quinoa with a fork and mix in the roasted vegetables. Sprinkle ground cumin over the top and serve.

MILLET WITH DATES AND ALMONDS

Ingredients

- Millet - 1 cup.
- Water - 2 cups.
- Dates - 1/2 cup, pitted and chopped.

- Almonds - 1/2 cup, sliced.
- Honey - 2 tbsp.
- Cinnamon - 1 tsp.
- Salt - a pinch.

Instructions

1. Rinse millet under cold water. In a pot, bring water to a boil. Add millet and salt, reduce heat to low, cover, and simmer for 20 minutes, or until water is absorbed.

2. Stir in dates, almonds, honey, and cinnamon. Cook for an additional 5 minutes.

3. Serve warm, drizzled with more honey if desired.

COUSCOUS WITH CHICKEN AND APRICOTS

Ingredients

- Couscous - 2 cups.
- Chicken broth - 4 cups.
- Chicken breasts - 2, cut into bite-sized pieces.
- Dried apricots - 1/2 cup, chopped.
- Onion - 1, finely chopped.
- Garlic cloves - 2, minced.
- Almonds - 1/4 cup, slivered.
- Cinnamon - 1 tsp.
- Turmeric - 1/2 tsp.
- Olive oil - 2 tbsp.
- Salt and pepper to taste.
- Fresh cilantro - for garnish.

Instructions

1. In a large pot, heat olive oil over medium heat. Add

chicken, onion, and garlic, sauté until chicken is browned.

2. Stir in cinnamon, turmeric, salt, and pepper. Cook for 1 minute.

3. Add chicken broth and bring to a boil. Add couscous and dried apricots, reduce heat to low, cover, and simmer for 10-15 minutes, or until couscous is tender and chicken is cooked through.

4. Stir in slivered almonds, adjust seasoning if necessary, and garnish with fresh cilantro before serving.

SPICED RICE WITH RAISINS

Ingredients

- Basmati rice - 2 cups, rinsed.
- Water - 4 cups.
- Raisins - 1/2 cup.
- Onion - 1, finely chopped.
- Garlic cloves - 2, minced.
- Cardamom pods - 4.
- Cinnamon stick - 1.
- Cloves - 4.
- Olive oil - 2 tbsp.
- Salt to taste.

Instructions

1. In a large pot, heat olive oil over medium heat. Add onion and garlic, sauté until softened.

2. Add cardamom pods, cinnamon stick, cloves, and salt. Cook for 1 minute.

3. Add rice and water, bring to a boil. Reduce heat to low, cover, and simmer for 20 minutes, or until rice is tender and water is absorbed.

4. Stir in raisins, cover, and let sit for 5 minutes.

5. Remove cardamom pods, cinnamon stick, and cloves before serving.

COUSCOUS WITH GRILLED VEGETABLES

Ingredients

- Couscous - 2 cups.
- Vegetable broth - 4 cups.
- Zucchini - 1, sliced.
- Red bell pepper - 1, sliced.
- Yellow squash - 1, sliced.
- Eggplant - 1, sliced.
- Cherry tomatoes - 1 cup.
- Olive oil - 2 tbsp.
- Salt and pepper to taste.
- Fresh basil - 1/4 cup, chopped.

Instructions

1. Preheat grill to medium-high heat. Toss zucchini, bell pepper, yellow squash, eggplant, and cherry tomatoes with olive oil, salt, and pepper.

2. Grill vegetables until tender and slightly charred, about 3-4 minutes per side.

3. In a large saucepan, bring vegetable broth to a boil. Stir in couscous, cover, and remove from heat. Let stand for 5 minutes, then fluff with a fork.

4. Mix grilled vegetables and fresh basil into couscous. Adjust seasoning with salt and pepper. Serve warm or at room temperature.

RICE AND LENTIL PILAF

Ingredients

- Long grain rice - 1 cup.
- Brown lentils - 1 cup, rinsed.
- Onion - 1, finely chopped.
- Carrot - 1, grated.
- Vegetable broth - 4 cups.
- Cumin - 1 tsp.
- Allspice - 1/2 tsp.
- Olive oil - 2 tbsp.
- Salt and pepper to taste.

Instructions

1. In a large skillet, heat olive oil over medium heat. Add onion and carrot, cook until softened, about 5 minutes.

2. Add rice, lentils, cumin, allspice, salt, and pepper. Stir to combine.

3. Pour in vegetable broth and bring to a boil. Reduce heat to low, cover, and simmer for 20-25 minutes, or until liquid is absorbed and rice and lentils are tender.

4. Fluff pilaf with a fork before serving. Adjust seasoning if needed.

COUSCOUS WITH LAMB AND VEGETABLES

Ingredients

- Couscous - 2 cups.
- Lamb - 1 lb., cubed.
- Carrots - 2, diced.
- Zucchini - 2, diced.
- Onion - 1, chopped.
- Garlic cloves - 2, minced.
- Chicken broth - 4 cups.
- Tomato paste - 1 tbsp.
- Ras el hanout - 1 tsp.
- Salt and pepper to taste.
- Olive oil - 2 tbsp.

Instructions

1. In a large pot, heat olive oil over medium heat. Add lamb, onion, and garlic, cook until lamb is browned.

2. Stir in carrots, zucchini, tomato paste, ras el hanout, salt, and pepper. Cook for 5 minutes.

3. Add chicken broth and bring to a boil. Reduce heat to low, cover, and simmer for 30 minutes, or until lamb is tender.

4. In a separate pot, prepare couscous according to package instructions using water or additional chicken broth.

5. Serve lamb and vegetable mixture over couscous, garnished with fresh herbs if desired.

BULGUR SALAD WITH MINT AND POMEGRANATE

Ingredients

- Bulgur - 1 cup.
- Water - 2 cups.
- Pomegranate seeds - 1/2 cup.
- Fresh mint - 1/4 cup, chopped.
- Cucumber - 1, diced.
- Red onion - 1/4 cup, finely chopped.
- Lemon juice - 2 tbsp.
- Olive oil - 2 tbsp.
- Salt and pepper to taste.

Instructions

1. In a large bowl, pour boiling water over bulgur. Cover and let stand for 30 minutes, or until water is absorbed and bulgur is tender.

2. Fluff bulgur with a fork and allow to cool slightly.

3. Add pomegranate seeds, mint, cucumber, red onion, lemon juice, olive oil, salt, and pepper to the bulgur. Toss to combine.

4. Chill in the refrigerator for at least 1 hour before serving to allow flavors to meld.

PEARL COUSCOUS WITH HERBS

Ingredients

- Pearl couscous - 2 cups.
- Chicken broth - 4 cups.
- Fresh parsley - 1/4 cup, chopped.

- Fresh cilantro - 1/4 cup, chopped.
- Green onion - 1/4 cup, chopped.
- Lemon zest - from 1 lemon.
- Olive oil - 2 tbsp.
- Salt and pepper to taste.

Instructions

1. In a large saucepan, bring chicken broth to a boil. Add pearl couscous, reduce heat to low, cover, and simmer for 10-12 minutes, or until liquid is absorbed and couscous is tender.

2. Remove from heat and let stand for 5 minutes. Fluff couscous with a fork.

3. Stir in parsley, cilantro, green onion, lemon zest, olive oil, salt, and pepper.

4. Serve warm or at room temperature, adjusted with additional salt, pepper, or lemon juice to taste.

SAFFRON RICE

Ingredients

- Basmati rice - 2 cups.
- Chicken broth - 4 cups.
- Saffron threads - 1/4 tsp, soaked in 2 tbsp hot water.
- Butter - 2 tbsp.
- Salt - 1 tsp.
- Onion - 1, finely chopped.

Instructions

1. Rinse the basmati rice under cold water until the water

runs clear. Drain.

2. In a large saucepan, melt butter over medium heat. Add the chopped onion and sauté until translucent.

3. Add the rice to the pan and stir to coat with the butter and onions.

4. Pour in the chicken broth and add the saffron with its soaking water. Add salt.

5. Bring to a boil, then reduce the heat to low, cover, and simmer for 20 minutes or until the rice is tender and the liquid has been absorbed.

6. Fluff the rice with a fork before serving.

COUSCOUS WITH FISH AND CILANTRO

Ingredients

- Couscous - 2 cups.
- Fish stock - 4 cups.
- Firm white fish - 1 lb, cut into chunks.
- Cilantro - 1/2 cup, chopped.
- Garlic - 2 cloves, minced.
- Cherry tomatoes - 1 cup, halved.
- Olive oil - 2 tbsp.
- Paprika - 1 tsp.
- Salt and pepper to taste.

Instructions

1. Prepare the couscous according to package instructions using fish stock instead of water.

2. In a large skillet, heat the olive oil over medium heat. Add the garlic and sauté until fragrant.

3. Add the fish chunks to the skillet and season with paprika, salt, and pepper. Cook until the fish is opaque and cooked through.

4. Stir in the cherry tomatoes and cook for another 2 minutes, just until they start to soften.

5. Serve the fish and tomato mixture over the prepared couscous. Garnish with chopped cilantro.

RICE WITH CHICKPEAS AND HARISSA

Ingredients

- Long grain rice - 2 cups.
- Chickpeas - 1 can (15 oz), drained and rinsed.
- Harissa paste - 2 tbsp, adjust to taste.
- Onion - 1, diced.
- Chicken broth - 4 cups.
- Carrots - 2, diced.
- Cumin - 1 tsp.
- Olive oil - 2 tbsp.
- Salt and pepper to taste.

Instructions

1. In a large saucepan, heat olive oil over medium heat. Add the diced onion and carrots, sauté until softened.

2. Stir in the harissa paste and cumin, cook for 1 minute until fragrant.

3. Add the rice and chickpeas, stirring to coat with the

harissa and vegetable mixture.

4. Pour in the chicken broth and season with salt and pepper. Bring to a boil.

5. Reduce heat to low, cover, and simmer for 20 minutes or until the rice is tender and the liquid is absorbed.

6. Fluff the rice with a fork and serve.

WHEAT BERRIES WITH ROASTED PEPPERS

Ingredients

- Wheat berries - 1 cup.
- Water - 4 cups.
- Red bell peppers - 2, roasted, peeled, and chopped.
- Garlic - 1 clove, minced.
- Olive oil - 2 tbsp.
- Lemon juice - 1 tbsp.
- Salt and pepper to taste.
- Parsley - 1/4 cup, chopped.

Instructions

1. Rinse the wheat berries and drain. In a large saucepan, bring water to a boil. Add the wheat berries, reduce heat to low, cover, and simmer for about 1 hour or until tender. Drain any excess water.

2. In a large bowl, combine the cooked wheat berries, roasted red peppers, garlic, olive oil, lemon juice, salt, pepper, and parsley. Toss to combine.

3. Adjust seasoning to taste and serve at room temperature or chilled.

COUSCOUS WITH SAFFRON AND ALMONDS

Ingredients

- Couscous - 2 cups.
- Chicken broth - 4 cups.
- Saffron threads - 1/2 tsp, soaked in 2 tbsp warm water.
- Butter - 2 tbsp.
- Almonds - 1/2 cup, toasted and slivered.
- Salt - 1 tsp.
- Onion - 1, finely chopped.

Instructions

1. In a large saucepan, melt the butter over medium heat. Add the chopped onion and sauté until translucent.

2. Add the chicken broth, saffron with its soaking water, and salt to the saucepan. Bring to a boil.

3. Stir in the couscous, cover, and remove from heat. Let stand for 5 minutes, then fluff with a fork.

4. Stir in the toasted slivered almonds before serving.

DESSERTS

Tunisian desserts stand out for their distinctive qualities, offering a sweet finale to the culinary journey through Tunisia's rich gastronomic landscape. These delights are crafted from a variety of ingredients, including nuts, fruits, and honey, each contributing to the nutritional value and complexity of flavors. The versatility of Tunisian sweets is evident in their range, from the simplicity of fresh fruit to the sophistication of pastries like baklava, all infused with aromatic spices that elevate the dining experience.

These confections play more than just the role of a meal's endnote; they are a deep dive into Tunisia's cultural heritage and culinary artistry. The preparation of Tunisian desserts involves time-honored techniques and recipes passed down through generations, showcasing the country's love for blending texture, flavor, and nutritional elements. This aspect of Tunisian cuisine not only satisfies the sweet tooth but also enriches the diet with dishes that are thoughtfully balanced in terms of healthfulness.

Tunisian desserts are an integral part of a diet that values both wellness and indulgence. Their presence in Tunisian cuisine underlines a commitment to creating meals that are as nourishing as they are delightful, marrying tradition with a mindful approach to eating.

BAKLAVA

Ingredients

- Phyllo dough - 1 package, thawed.
- Unsalted butter - 1 cup, melted.

- Walnuts - 2 cups, finely chopped.
- Sugar - 1/2 cup.
- Cinnamon - 1 tsp.
- For the syrup:
- Water - 1 cup.
- Sugar - 1 cup.
- Honey - 1/2 cup.
- Lemon juice - 1 tbsp.
- Vanilla extract - 1 tsp.

Instructions

1. Preheat oven to 350°F (175°C).

2. Mix walnuts, sugar, and cinnamon in a bowl. Set aside.

3. Brush the bottom and sides of a 9x13 inch baking dish with melted butter. Place one sheet of phyllo dough in the dish, brush with melted butter, and repeat with 8 more sheets.

4. Sprinkle a thin layer of the walnut mixture over the phyllo. Cover with two more sheets of phyllo, buttering each sheet. Repeat the layers until all the walnut mixture is used, finishing with a top layer of 8-10 sheets of buttered phyllo.

5. Cut the baklava into diamonds or squares before baking.

6. Bake for 50 minutes, or until golden and crisp.

7. While baklava is baking, make the syrup by boiling water and sugar until sugar is dissolved. Add honey and lemon juice, simmer for about 20 minutes. Stir in vanilla.

8. Remove baklava from oven and immediately pour the syrup over it. Let cool completely before serving.

MAKROUD

Ingredients

- Semolina - 2 cups.
- Butter - 1/2 cup, melted.
- Water - 3/4 cup.
- For the filling:
- Dates - 1 cup, pitted and mashed.
- Cinnamon - 1/2 tsp.
- Orange blossom water - 1 tbsp.
- For frying:
- Vegetable oil.
- For the syrup:
- Honey - 1 cup.
- Orange blossom water - 1 tbsp.

Instructions

1. Mix semolina and melted butter in a bowl. Gradually add water until a dough forms. Let rest for 1 hour.

2. For the filling, mix dates, cinnamon, and orange blossom water.

3. Divide the dough into small balls. Flatten each ball, place a spoonful of date filling in the center, and fold the dough over to encase the filling. Shape into a diamond or rectangle.

4. Heat oil in a deep fryer or large saucepan. Fry the makroud until golden brown.

5. Warm the honey and mix with orange blossom water. Dip the fried makroud in the honey mixture and let soak for a few minutes before removing to a wire rack to drain.

6. Serve once cooled.

TUNISIAN DATE CAKE

Ingredients

- Dates - 1 cup, pitted and chopped.
- Boiling water - 1 cup.
- Flour - 1 3/4 cups.
- Baking soda - 1 tsp.
- Salt - 1/2 tsp.
- Butter - 1/2 cup, softened.
- Sugar - 1 cup.
- Eggs - 2.
- Vanilla extract - 1 tsp.
- Walnuts - 1/2 cup, chopped.

Instructions

1. Preheat oven to 350°F (175°C). Grease and flour a 9-inch cake pan.

2. Pour boiling water over chopped dates and let sit for 10 minutes. Drain any excess water.

3. In a bowl, mix flour, baking soda, and salt.

4. In another bowl, cream together butter and sugar. Beat in eggs, one at a time, then stir in vanilla.

5. Blend in the flour mixture. Fold in the moist dates and walnuts.

6. Pour batter into the prepared pan.

7. Bake for 40-45 minutes or until a toothpick inserted into the center comes out clean. Let cool before serving.

ASSIDA

Ingredients

- Semolina - 2 cups.
- Water - 6 cups.
- Salt - 1 tsp.
- Butter - 1/4 cup.
- Honey or olive oil for serving.

Instructions

1. In a large pot, bring water to a boil. Add salt.

2. Gradually whisk in the semolina. Reduce heat to low and cook, stirring constantly, until the mixture thickens and pulls away from the sides of the pot, about 15-20 minutes.

3. Stir in butter until melted and well incorporated.

4. Spoon the Assida into bowls. Serve with honey or olive oil on top.

YOYO (TUNISIAN DOUGHNUTS)

Ingredients

- All-purpose flour - 2 cups.
- Baking powder - 1 tsp.
- Sugar - 1/2 cup.
- Eggs - 2.
- Orange zest - from 1 orange.
- Orange juice - 1/4 cup.
- Vegetable oil for frying.
- Sugar for coating.

Instructions

1. In a bowl, mix flour, baking powder, and sugar.

2. Beat in eggs, orange zest, and orange juice until a soft dough forms.

3. Heat oil in a deep fryer or large saucepan to 375°F (190°C).

4. Drop spoonfuls of dough into the hot oil and fry until golden brown.

5. Remove with a slotted spoon and drain on paper towels.

6. While still warm, roll the doughnuts in sugar to coat.

7. Serve warm or at room temperature.

BJAOUIYA (NUT-FILLED PASTRIES)

Ingredients

- Phyllo dough - 10 sheets.
- Mixed nuts (almonds, pistachios, walnuts) - 2 cups, finely chopped.
- Sugar - 1/2 cup.
- Cinnamon - 1 tsp.
- Butter - 1/2 cup, melted.
- For the syrup:
- Sugar - 1 cup.
- Water - 1/2 cup.
- Lemon juice - 1 tbsp.
- Rose water - 1 tsp.

Instructions

1. Preheat oven to 350°F (175°C).

2. Combine the nuts, sugar, and cinnamon in a bowl.

3. Brush a sheet of phyllo dough with melted butter, place another sheet on top, and brush again. Cut into squares or rectangles.

4. Place a spoonful of the nut mixture on each piece of dough. Fold and roll to enclose the filling.

5. Arrange the pastries on a baking sheet. Brush the tops with more melted butter.

6. Bake for 20-25 minutes, until golden brown.

7. Meanwhile, make the syrup by boiling the sugar and water until thickened. Add the lemon juice and rose water.

8. Pour the hot syrup over the baked pastries. Let cool before serving.

SAMSA (ALMOND AND SESAME PASTRIES)

Ingredients

- Filo pastry - 1 package.
- Almonds - 2 cups, ground.
- Sugar - 3/4 cup.
- Butter - 1/2 cup, melted.
- Cinnamon - 1 tsp.
- Orange flower water - 2 tbsp.
- Sesame seeds - 1/2 cup, for coating.
- Honey - for glazing.

Instructions

1. Preheat oven to 350°F (175°C).

2. Mix ground almonds, sugar, cinnamon, and orange flower water in a bowl.

3. Cut filo pastry into strips, brush with melted butter, and place a spoonful of the almond mixture at one end.

4. Fold the pastry over the filling to form a triangle, continuing to fold until the strip is used up.

5. Brush the outside with butter and coat with sesame seeds.

6. Place on a baking sheet and bake for 15-20 minutes, until golden.

7. Warm honey in a saucepan and brush over the pastries while still hot. Let cool before serving.

GHRAIBA (TUNISIAN SHORTBREAD)

Ingredients

- Chickpea flour - 2 cups.
- Butter - 1 cup, softened.
- Powdered sugar - 1 cup.
- Vanilla extract - 1 tsp.
- Salt - a pinch.

Instructions

1. Preheat oven to 325°F (160°C).

2. Cream the butter and powdered sugar together until

light and fluffy. Add vanilla extract and salt.

3. Gradually add chickpea flour to the butter mixture, mixing until a dough forms.

4. Roll dough into small balls and place on a baking sheet. Flatten slightly.

5. Bake for 10-15 minutes, or until lightly golden. Let cool on the baking sheet before transferring to a wire rack.

MHALBI (RICE PUDDING)

Ingredients

- Rice flour - 1/2 cup.
- Milk - 4 cups.
- Sugar - 1/2 cup.
- Rose water - 2 tbsp.
- Ground cinnamon - for garnish.
- Chopped nuts (almonds, pistachios) - for garnish.

Instructions

1. In a saucepan, mix rice flour with a little milk to make a smooth paste.

2. Add the rest of the milk and sugar, whisking constantly to prevent lumps.

3. Cook over medium heat, stirring constantly, until the mixture thickens and comes to a boil.

4. Remove from heat and stir in rose water.

5. Pour into serving dishes and refrigerate until set.

6. Garnish with ground cinnamon and chopped nuts before serving.

ZRIR (SESAME AND HONEY PASTE)

Ingredients

- Sesame seeds - 1 cup, toasted.
- Honey - 1/2 cup.
- Butter - 2 tbsp.
- Almonds - 1/4 cup, toasted and chopped.

Instructions

1. In a food processor, blend the toasted sesame seeds until they form a paste.

2. In a saucepan, heat the honey and butter together until the butter melts and the mixture is well combined.

3. Add the sesame paste and chopped almonds to the honey mixture. Stir until well combined and heated through.

4. Pour the mixture into a greased dish or mold. Allow to cool and set before slicing.

5. Serve as a sweet snack or dessert.

TUNISIAN ORANGE CAKE

Ingredients

- Flour - 2 cups.
- Sugar - 1 cup.
- Baking powder - 2 tsp.
- Salt - 1/2 tsp.

- Oranges - 2, juiced and zested.
- Vegetable oil - 1/2 cup.
- Eggs - 4.
- For the syrup:
- Orange juice - 1/2 cup (from oranges).
- Sugar - 1/4 cup.

Instructions

1. Preheat the oven to 350°F (175°C). Grease and flour a 9-inch round cake pan.

2. In a bowl, mix together flour, sugar, baking powder, and salt.

3. In another bowl, combine orange juice, zest, vegetable oil, and eggs. Beat until smooth.

4. Gradually add the wet ingredients to the dry ingredients, mixing until just combined.

5. Pour the batter into the prepared cake pan and bake for about 30 minutes, or until a toothpick inserted into the center comes out clean.

6. While the cake is baking, prepare the syrup by heating the orange juice and sugar in a small saucepan over medium heat until the sugar dissolves.

7. Once the cake is done, remove from the oven and while still warm, poke holes in the top with a fork and pour the syrup over the cake.

8. Allow the cake to cool completely before serving.

KAAK WARKA (ALMOND COOKIES)

Ingredients

- Almonds - 2 cups, ground.
- Sugar - 1 cup.
- Egg whites - 3.
- Rose water - 1 tbsp.
- Icing sugar - for dusting.

Instructions

1. Preheat the oven to 325°F (165°C). Line a baking sheet with parchment paper.

2. In a bowl, mix together the ground almonds and sugar.

3. Add the egg whites and rose water, and stir until a thick dough forms.

4. Take small amounts of dough and roll into balls. Place on the prepared baking sheet.

5. Bake for 10-15 minutes, or until the cookies are firm to the touch.

6. Remove from the oven and while still warm, dust with icing sugar.

7. Allow to cool on the baking sheet before serving.

HARISSA (SEMOLINA AND ALMOND CAKE)

Ingredients

- Semolina - 2 cups.
- Sugar - 1 cup.

- Butter - 1 cup, melted.
- Almonds - 1 cup, ground.
- Baking powder - 1 tsp.
- Yogurt - 1 cup.
- For the syrup:
- Water - 1 cup.
- Sugar - 1 cup.
- Lemon juice - 1 tbsp.

Instructions

1. Preheat the oven to 350°F (175°C). Grease and flour a 9x13 inch baking dish.

2. In a large bowl, mix together semolina, sugar, melted butter, ground almonds, baking powder, and yogurt until well combined.

3. Spread the mixture into the prepared baking dish and bake for 30-35 minutes, or until golden brown.

4. While the cake is baking, prepare the syrup by boiling water, sugar, and lemon juice in a small saucepan over medium heat until the sugar dissolves and the syrup thickens slightly.

5. Once the cake is done, remove from the oven and immediately pour the hot syrup over the hot cake.

6. Allow the cake to cool completely in the dish before cutting into squares and serving.

FEKKAS (RUSK WITH ALMONDS)

Ingredients

- Flour - 4 cups.

- Sugar - 1 cup.
- Butter - 1 cup, softened.
- Almonds - 1 cup, whole.
- Eggs - 2.
- Baking powder - 2 tsp.
- Orange flower water - 2 tbsp.
- Sesame seeds - 2 tbsp.

Instructions

1. Preheat the oven to 350°F (175°C).

2. In a large bowl, cream together butter and sugar. Beat in eggs one at a time.

3. Stir in orange flower water.

4. In another bowl, sift together flour and baking powder. Gradually add to the wet ingredients until a dough forms.

5. Fold in whole almonds and sesame seeds.

6. Divide the dough into logs and place on a baking sheet. Bake for 25-30 minutes, until golden.

7. Remove from oven, cool slightly, and slice diagonally into 1/2 inch slices.

8. Return slices to the oven and bake for an additional 10-15 minutes, until crisp and golden.

9. Cool completely before serving.

MASFOUF (SWEET COUSCOUS)

Ingredients

- Couscous - 2 cups.
- Butter - 1/4 cup, melted.
- Water - 2 cups.
- Sugar - 1/2 cup, or to taste.
- Raisins - 1/2 cup.
- Almonds - 1/4 cup, blanched and chopped.
- Pomegranate seeds - 1/4 cup.
- Rose water - 1 tbsp (optional).

Instructions

1. Prepare the couscous according to package instructions, fluffing it with the melted butter once cooked.

2. Boil the water and pour over the couscous. Cover and let sit for 5 minutes, then fluff with a fork.

3. Stir in sugar, raisins, almonds, and pomegranate seeds. Sprinkle with rose water if using.

4. Serve warm or at room temperature, adjusted with more sugar if desired.

BOUZA (HAZELNUT CREAM DESSERT)

Ingredients

- Hazelnuts - 2 cups, roasted and ground.
- Milk - 4 cups.
- Cornstarch - 1/4 cup.
- Sugar - 1/2 cup.
- Rose water - 1 tbsp.

- Whipped cream - for garnish.
- Ground cinnamon - for garnish.

Instructions

1. In a medium saucepan, mix the milk, cornstarch, and sugar until the cornstarch is completely dissolved.

2. Add the ground hazelnuts to the saucepan and mix well.

3. Cook over medium heat, stirring constantly, until the mixture thickens and begins to bubble.

4. Remove from heat and stir in the rose water.

5. Pour the mixture into serving bowls and refrigerate until set, about 2 hours.

6. Garnish with whipped cream and a sprinkle of ground cinnamon before serving.

TUNISIAN ALMOND AND PISTACHIO BAKLAVA

Ingredients

- Phyllo dough - 1 package, thawed.
- Unsalted butter - 1 cup, melted.
- Almonds - 1 cup, finely chopped.
- Pistachios - 1 cup, finely chopped.
- Sugar - 1/2 cup.
- Cinnamon - 1 tsp.
- For the syrup:
- Water - 1 cup.
- Sugar - 1 cup.
- Honey - 1/2 cup.

- Orange blossom water - 1 tbsp.
- Lemon juice - 1 tbsp.

Instructions

1. Preheat oven to 350°F (175°C).

2. Brush a 9x13 inch baking dish with melted butter. Place one sheet of phyllo dough in the dish, brush with melted butter, and repeat with 8 more sheets.

3. Mix the almonds, pistachios, sugar, and cinnamon in a bowl. Sprinkle a third of the nut mixture over the phyllo in the dish.

4. Layer 5 more sheets of phyllo, buttering each sheet. Add another third of the nut mixture. Repeat with 5 more sheets and the remaining nut mixture, finishing with a top layer of 8-10 sheets of buttered phyllo.

5. Using a sharp knife, cut the baklava into diamond or square shapes.

6. Bake for about 50 minutes, or until golden and crisp.

7. While the baklava is baking, make the syrup by combining water, sugar, honey, orange blossom water, and lemon juice in a saucepan. Bring to a boil, then simmer for about 20 minutes.

8. Pour the hot syrup over the hot baklava as soon as it comes out of the oven. Let cool completely before serving.

LOUKOUM (TURKISH DELIGHT)

Ingredients

- Sugar - 4 cups.
- Water - 4 1/2 cups.
- Cornstarch - 1 cup.
- Lemon juice - 1 tbsp.
- Rose water - 2 tbsp.
- Food coloring (optional) - a few drops.
- Icing sugar - for dusting.

Instructions

1. In a large saucepan, combine 4 cups of water, sugar, and lemon juice. Stir over low heat until the sugar dissolves.

2. In a separate bowl, mix the cornstarch with 1/2 cup of water until smooth. Gradually add to the sugar mixture, stirring constantly.

3. Cook over low heat, stirring constantly, until the mixture thickens and becomes translucent.

4. Remove from heat and stir in the rose water and food coloring if using.

5. Pour the mixture into a greased pan and let cool until set.

6. Once set, cut into cubes and dust with icing sugar to prevent sticking.

7. Store in an airtight container.

QALB EL LOUZ
(SEMOLINA AND ALMOND DESSERT)

Ingredients

- Semolina - 2 cups.
- Sugar - 1 cup.
- Butter - 1 cup, melted.
- Almonds - 1/2 cup, blanched and chopped.
- Water - 2 cups.
- Orange blossom water - 2 tbsp.
- For the syrup:
- Sugar - 2 cups.
- Water - 1 cup.
- Lemon juice - 1 tbsp.

Instructions

1. Preheat oven to 350°F (175°C).

2. In a bowl, mix semolina, sugar, and melted butter until well combined. Press half of the mixture into a greased baking dish.

3. Sprinkle the chopped almonds over the semolina layer. Cover with the remaining semolina mixture, pressing down gently.

4. Cut into diamond shapes and bake for 35-40 minutes, or until golden brown.

5. While the dessert is baking, prepare the syrup by boiling the sugar, water, and lemon juice until thickened.

6. Pour the hot syrup over the hot dessert as soon as it comes out of the oven. Let cool completely before serving.

TUNISIAN LEMON SORBET

Ingredients

- Lemons - 6, juiced.
- Water - 3 cups.
- Sugar - 1 cup.
- Lemon zest - from 2 lemons.

Instructions

1. In a saucepan, combine the water and sugar. Heat over medium heat, stirring until the sugar dissolves.

2. Remove from heat and add the lemon juice and zest. Stir to combine.

3. Chill the mixture in the refrigerator until cold.

4. Once chilled, pour the mixture into an ice cream maker and churn according to the manufacturer's instructions.

5. Transfer the sorbet to a freezer-safe container and freeze until firm.

6. Serve in chilled bowls or glasses.

RECIPE LIST

SPICES & PANTRY

HARISSA	10
RAS EL HANOUT	10
TABIL	11
CHERMOULA	11
BZAR (TUNISIAN SPICE MIX)	12
DRIED MINT	13
CARAWAY POWDER	13
CORIANDER SEEDS	14
SMEN (CLARIFIED BUTTER)	14
PRESERVED LEMONS	15

APPETIZERS

BRIK À L'ŒUF	16
MECHOUIA SALAD	17
TUNISIAN FELFEL	18
ZAALOUK	19
LABLABI	20
TUNISIAN SAMSA	20
KAFTEJI	21
MERGUEZ SAUSAGE	22
TUNISIAN BOUREK	22
HMISS	23
MAKROUD EL LOUSE	24
TAKTOUKA	24

CHAKCHOUKA 25
TUNISIAN FALAFEL 26
OJJA (WITH MERGUEZ) 27

SALADS

SALAD TUNISIENNE 29
CARROT SALAD WITH CUMIN 30
BEETROOT SALAD 31
TUNA AND EGG SALAD 31
CUCUMBER AND YOGURT SALAD 32
ORANGE AND OLIVE SALAD 33
GRILLED VEGETABLE SALAD 33
POTATO AND OLIVE SALAD 34
CABBAGE SALAD 35
FATTOUSH TUNISIAN STYLE 36
EGGPLANT SALAD 37
ARTICHOKE SALAD 37
SLICED TOMATO AND ONION SALAD 38
RADISH AND MINT SALAD 39
SPICY CARROT AND CHICKPEA SALAD 39

SOUPS

CHORBA FRIK 41
LABLABI (CHICKPEA SOUP) 42
HARIRA 43
BISSARA (FAVA BEAN SOUP) 44
LENTIL SOUP 45

PUMPKIN SOUP WITH HARISSA 46

BARLEY SOUP 47

FISH SOUP 48

TOMATO AND BREAD SOUP 48

MEATBALL AND VEGETABLE SOUP.............................. 49

CHICKEN AND RICE SOUP.. 50

SEAFOOD BISQUE 51

SPINACH AND LENTIL SOUP 52

SORGHUM SOUP 53

CARROT AND CORIANDER SOUP................................. 54

STEWS

MARQA (TUNISIAN STEW) 55

OJJA WITH SEAFOOD.. 56

LAMB AND VEGETABLE TAGINE 57

CHICKEN AND CHICKPEA STEW................................... 58

BEEF AND PRUNE STEW 59

FISH AND POTATO STEW... 60

SPINACH AND MEAT STEW.. 61

ARTICHOKE AND PEA STEW.. 62

SQUID AND TOMATO STEW.. 63

PUMPKIN AND LAMB STEW 64

CHAKCHOUKA WITH MEAT 65

EGGPLANT AND BEEF STEW 66

TUNISIAN RATATOUILLE.. 67

OKRA AND TOMATO STEW 68

MLOUKHIYA (JUTE LEAVES STEW) 69

SEAFOOD

GRILLED SARDINES 70
BAKED SEA BREAM WITH HARISSA 71
TUNISIAN FISH TAGINE 72
CALAMARI IN TOMATO SAUCE 73
STUFFED MACKEREL 74
GRILLED SEA BASS 75
SPICY FISH SOUP 76
ANCHOVY AND EGG SALAD 77
MUSSELS IN SPICY BROTH 77
TUNA STUFFED PEPPERS 78
SEAFOOD GRATIN 79
FISH BALLS IN TOMATO SAUCE 80
SEAFOOD OJJA 81
SQUID STUFFED WITH RICE 82
FRIED FISH WITH HARISSA SAUCE 83

POULTRY

CHICKEN COUSCOUS 84
ROASTED CHICKEN WITH PRESERVED LEMON 86
TUNISIAN CHICKEN TAGINE 87
CHICKEN WITH OLIVES AND CAPERS 88
STUFFED CHICKEN WITH FREEKEH 89
GRILLED CHICKEN WITH HARISSA 90
CHICKEN AND ALMOND BRIK 91
TUNISIAN CHICKEN KEBABS 92
CHICKEN LIVER WITH HARISSA ON TOAST 93

CHICKEN AND EGGPLANT STEW 93
CHICKEN MLOUKHIYA 94
TUNISIAN CHICKEN WITH APRICOTS 95
CHICKEN SHAWARMA TUNISIAN STYLE 96
ROASTED DUCK WITH DATES 97
CHICKEN AND FIG TAGINE 98
CHICKEN PASTILLA 99
CHICKEN WITH CHICKPEAS AND HARISSA 100
TUNISIAN JERK CHICKEN 101
CHICKEN AND POTATO GRATIN 102
CHICKEN WITH PRESERVED LEMON, OLIVES 103

LAMB DISHES

LAMB COUSCOUS 104
GRILLED LAMB CHOPS WITH HARISSA 105
LAMB SHANK TAGINE 106
SPICED LAMB KEBABS 107
LAMB MLOUKHIYA 108
LAMB AND PRUNE STEW 109
ROASTED LAMB SHOULDER WITH ROSEMARY 110
LAMB AND CHICKPEA STEW 111
LAMB TAGINE WITH APRICOTS 112
LAMB SAUSAGE WITH HARISSA 113
LAMB MEATBALLS IN TOMATO SAUCE 113
STUFFED LAMB WITH RICE AND NUTS 114
LAMB AND SPINACH STEW 115
LAMB SHANK WITH SAFFRON 116

BRAISED LAMB WITH FENNEL 117

LAMB BRIK 118

LAMB WITH ARTICHOKES AND PEAS 119

LAMB LIVER WITH SPICES 120

GRILLED LAMB WITH MINT 121

LAMB AND EGGPLANT TAGINE 121

BEEF DISHES

BEEF COUSCOUS 123

TUNISIAN BEEF STEW 124

BEEF TAGINE WITH POTATOES 125

SPICY BEEF WITH VEGETABLES 126

BEEF AND BARLEY SOUP 127

BEEF KEBABS WITH HARISSA 128

BEEF BRIK 129

BEEF AND CARROT STEW 130

MEATBALL TAGINE WITH EGGS 130

BEEF LIVER WITH CUMIN 131

STUFFED BEEF ROLLS 132

BEEF AND TURNIP STEW 133

BEEF SAUSAGE IN TOMATO SAUCE 134

GRILLED BEEF WITH SPICES 134

BEEF WITH DRIED FRUITS 135

BEEF MLOUKHIYA 136

BEEF PASTILLA 137

BRAISED BEEF WITH ONIONS 138

BEEF AND PUMPKIN TAGINE 139

BEEF WITH GREEN BEANS AND TOMATOES 140

GRAIN DISHES

TRADITIONAL TUNISIAN COUSCOUS 141
FREEKEH WITH LAMB 142
BARLEY PILAF 143
TUNISIAN RICE PILAF 144
BULGUR WITH VEGETABLES 145
COUSCOUS WITH SEAFOOD 146
QUINOA WITH ROASTED VEGETABLES 147
MILLET WITH DATES AND ALMONDS 147
COUSCOUS WITH CHICKEN AND APRICOTS 148
SPICED RICE WITH RAISINS 149
COUSCOUS WITH GRILLED VEGETABLES 150
RICE AND LENTIL PILAF 151
COUSCOUS WITH LAMB AND VEGETABLES 152
BULGUR SALAD WITH MINT, POMEGRANATE 153
PEARL COUSCOUS WITH HERBS 153
SAFFRON RICE 154
COUSCOUS WITH FISH AND CILANTRO 155
RICE WITH CHICKPEAS AND HARISSA 156
WHEAT BERRIES WITH ROASTED PEPPERS 157
COUSCOUS WITH SAFFRON AND ALMONDS 158

DESSERTS

BAKLAVA 159
MAKROUD 161

TUNISIAN DATE CAKE	162
ASSIDA	163
YOYO (TUNISIAN DOUGHNUTS)	163
BJAOUIYA (NUT-FILLED PASTRIES)	164
SAMSA (ALMOND AND SESAME PASTRIES)	165
GHRAIBA (TUNISIAN SHORTBREAD)	166
MHALBI (RICE PUDDING)	167
ZRIR (SESAME AND HONEY PASTE)	168
TUNISIAN ORANGE CAKE	168
KAAK WARKA (ALMOND COOKIES)	170
HARISSA (SEMOLINA AND ALMOND CAKE)	170
FEKKAS (RUSK WITH ALMONDS)	171
MASFOUF (SWEET COUSCOUS)	173
BOUZA (HAZELNUT CREAM DESSERT)	173
TUNISIAN ALMOND AND PISTACHIO BAKLAVA	174
LOUKOUM (TURKISH DELIGHT)	176
QALB EL LOUZ	177
TUNISIAN LEMON SORBET	178

Printed in Great Britain
by Amazon